Acknowledgements and Gratitude

I would like to first express my gratitude towards my Writers' Group members, Donelle, Gail, Nancy, Stephen and Sue for their encouragement and loving, if not relentless, critiques of my work. Your support is as infinite as your personal talents.

Thank you to my editors Stephanie and Larry. It is only because of your eyes for detail this story has come together. Your acumen for formatting and unwavering patience have been the filling and the icing that has brought this project to fruition.

Beyond the echoes of clanking dishes and clinking glasses is my heartfelt gratitude to my Friends Amid Food. Whether you are working with staple ingredients or scarce and unusual aromatics, no matter what's on the oven in the stove or atop the grill, your creations carry those fortunate enough to sit at your table, to exotic destinations and back to the comforts of home and hearth. From micro-brewed beers concocted in your garage, to everything drizzled with syrup, from basic French *cassoulet* to the surreal actualization of a molecular gastronomic foam, my Friends can always be counted on to offer up a memorable food experience. Thank you for your friendship and collaboration as well as providing a cornucopia of fodder for my writing.

It is equally important I extend sincere thanks to those surgeons who took the time to answer my elementary questions and gave detailed explanations of the types of weight loss surgery options available as well as their enthusiasm and promotion for this project. In addition, I must recognize the time given to me by those many patients who openly shared their personal experiences before the surgery and afterward. Always speaking with brutal honesty about obesity, the never ending cycles of weight gain and loss, as well as your feelings, concerns and hopes for the future. Your stories always, without failure, touched my heart. I feel fortunate that it was me you chose to share them with. The vulnerability of these individuals during our time together moved me deeply. I can't thank them enough.

Also I must give recognition to my four children. All of whom took the time to read, re-read then listen to me read, my writings. They then gave relevant, serious yet loving feedback on every version of this book. Especially Addison, who has had to talk me off the cliff countless times, then seat himself at my computer to fix and figure out the messes I created.

Finally, it is with a Bear's hug (she knows what I mean) that I thank my little sister for her lighting of the spark and her ongoing stoking and kindling of this book's birth and completion. While we may not look exactly alike and the foods we eat don't show up the same way, we do share the same laugh and sense of humor. We take great delight in watching cooking shows together, preparing meals then sitting down with family to enjoy them. I am lucky to experience the unique connection that only sisters can have. Thank you Sis for everything you have done and everything you are.

INTRODUCTION

It is with compassion and personal understanding that I write this story-cookbook for those of us who have, sometimes unclear, but always evident, deep-seated reasons for overeating, bingeing, purging, and dieting. The reasons we engage in these circuitous behaviors are as varied as the choices displayed in a bakery display case, the outcomes, not so much. That is, a predictable cycle of weight loss, weight gain, weight loss, weight gain, weight loss. At the very heart of this book is an acknowledgment and appreciation that for most of us food consumption extends beyond eating solely for nourishment. We eat in connection with family gatherings, social events, in loneliness, in boredom and in celebration. So how does one balance the scale?

Five years ago I found myself standing in line for something I rarely stand in line for, or even really enjoy, a buffet line. The muffled echoes of clattering dishes and glasses clanging against one

 another amid sounds of disconnected conversations muscled their way into my ears. As I looked past the people in front of me, oversized counters peered out from beneath their visors known as "sneeze guards," displaying a smorgasbord of foods from all around the world. Drawing on my own experience traveling abroad, I don't recall the meals I've feasted upon resembling in the least the spread of epicurean diversity arranged in towers, pyramids and flowing edible waterfalls that surrounded me. I also noticed there didn't seem to be any distinct aroma emanating from the seven corners of the world where I currently stood. Rather, this melting pot of ethnicity situated in a massive dining room emitted a nondescript scent similar to a misting system of muddled infusions. Rays of baguettes arranged like flower bouquets, meats, seafood, pastas and filtered cigarette smoke were mingled and tangled together riding on a magic carpet of air conditioning. I didn't find it pleasing.

But I was with friends and the majority ruled, so there I waited with cash in hand. Finally, I moved up to second in line. My friends waited for me off to the side as I'd inadvertently lost my original place while taking in the sights. Mindful of personal space, I still couldn't help overhearing the couple in front of me ask the hostess if this buffet offered discounts to people who've had gastric bypass.

What?! Weight-loss surgery! Discounts? I stepped up a little closer. The husband (or so I presumed him to be) went on to explain to the hostess, who wore an expression of confusion, that some of the local hotel-casinos give discounts or charge only the cost of a child's plate to those who've undergone weight-loss surgery. I guess he thought using a different term would help the hostess understand. I watched as she slowly shook her head from side to side wearing a puzzled expression. I, on the other hand, knew exactly what gastric bypass was, though I'd never heard of such discounts. *Was there some kind of medical card or special I.D. these patients carried?*

It just so happened I was in the middle of researching my idea for this very project, a cookbook of recipes specifically for those who have had weight-loss surgery! After the shock of my great luck to be standing near this man and his wife passed, I wondered, *if they can only eat four ounces of food at any meal, as is the norm following such procedures. What on earth are they doing at a buffet?* But I knew. I knew exactly why this couple had stood in line behind so many others to purchase their tickets for entry into this carnival of food. My instincts for writing this recipe-story book were correct. I casually leaned in further as the man continued speaking to the hostess now asking for a manager. I knew exactly why they were there. They can't help themselves. This couple, like so many others, are still drawn in to the sights and sounds of food. The urge to eat is overwhelming. He could see she still had no idea what he was talking about. The man and his wife stepped aside, and I was called up by the hostess to buy my own ticket. My head was spinning with excitement. The scene that had just played out in front of me was a sign, a message telling me I was on the right track. Certainly I was at the right buffet.

I originally came up with the idea for this book when prompted by a simple request made by my sister. The seed she planted bloomed in my head like yeast in sugar water, and continued to take shape as I began introducing myself to a number of complete strangers who were willing to share their personal stories on the topic. Their struggles with weight, which in many cases they had their entire lives, frustrations and disappointments. Their hopes prior to, and concerns having bariatric amendments often turned into sessions lasting hours. Most had not felt safe or permitted to spend any real time talking candidly with a willing listener. Feeling encouraged to pursue my research I went on to interview surgeons and nutritionists. I began attending meetings led by facilitators who provide support and guidance, in addition to selling food supplements, to patients in the weeks following their surgery.

All those I approached expressed sincere interest and enthusiasm regarding a cookbook they could use that would provide them with recipes measured in serving sizes equal to their intake capabilities, foods they could consume without discomfort or pain afterward. Even better - a recipe book to feed their hungry souls - appease the culinary adventurer within, or simply engage their love of food and food stories. During these months of research, I was thrilled to learn I am not the only one who collects and reads cookbooks and diet books as though they were the best fiction ever written.

While weight-loss surgery does indeed serve as a deterrent or even arrest the further development of illnesses and other ailments related to carrying excessive weight, the surgery itself does little to address our mental and emotional relationships with food. But this book, One 4-Ounce Serving, does. More importantly, the recipes in this book will serve not only those with dietary restrictions or portion limitations but also those who don't.

As for the food stories, they serve to celebrate the fulfillment and joy we food lovers feel when preparing and serving food, whether dining alone or in the jovial company of friends and family.

Food for Thought or is it Thoughts of Food?

Rose walked into the contemporary, sleek, almost industrial-looking state room with the low-back sofa and reflective picture frames displaying schmears and splatters of paint. The early morning sun streamed in through the sliding glass door, but her eyes were immediately drawn to a fragmented arrangement of doughnuts sitting on a room service tray. Each doughnut lay sadly impaired and disfigured, a mangled bite ripped from one of its glazed, powered or sprinkled and rounded sides. Standing next to the dozen or so doughnuts was a half full glass of orange juice, on the television played a *King Of Queens* rerun. This caught Rose's attention for a moment as it was one of her favorite episodes, the one where Doug teaches Carrie how to pole dance. In spite of this evidence of recent activity there didn't appear to be anyone in the room.

Rose stood in the small, rectangular doorway, trying to make sense of the surreal scene before her. It felt as though she was experiencing a kind of ethereal moment when once familiar surroundings slide into a thick haze and become a freeze-frame of time. This prompted her to remember yet another scene from one of her favorite books. Upon waking, the main character shuffled to the bathroom, then opened and reached into the medicine cabinet for his toothbrush. He detected nothing extraordinary this particular morning until he brushed the sleep from his blurry eyes. As he pulled back the mirrored door, he was stunned to see the shelves inside were all slightly askew. Jolted by this unexpected sight, he quickly slammed the door shut. He inhaled deeply, closed his eyes tightly, giving them time to adjust. Now fully awake, ever so slowly he reopened the door just a crack, peering inside to see if this altered version of reality had truly occurred. Yes, the cabinet shelves were definitely still slanted. Deodorant, cologne and other items that just yesterday were so neatly arranged now jumbled together at one end. He stood in wonder.

The scene in this novel is a poignant one for Rose since her sister swears she saw the tooth fairy in their family medicine cabinet one morning when she opened the door to reach for her toothbrush. Gilda was about five years old at the time. Yet even now as an adult, Gilda holds this story to be true. Whenever Gilda is asked to retell her tooth fairy story, she explains that when discovered the tooth fairy emitted a high-pitched squeal. Gilda immediately slammed the door shut, slowly reopened it so as not to frighten the fairy again, but the fairy had already disappeared. Gilda always drops her voice at this point of the story clearly reliving the sadness and disappointment she felt as a child.

Rose retreated backward a couple of steps, paused, then tilted her head from one side to the other. Yes, the predicament of the scattered doughnuts was unchanged.

Snapping her from her thoughts Rose heard sounds of retching and vomiting coming through the closed door of the bathroom. She realized it was her sister.

"Gilda? Gilda, are you alright?" Rose called out. "Gilda! Let me in!" Rose shouted at the door.

"It's open, you idiot!" Gilda gagged back.

Opening the door, Rose saw Gilda scrunched up in the small bathroom quarters, bent over the toilet.

"Oh no, what can I do to help?" Rose asked, ignoring her sister's offending adjective.

"I need a wet washcloth." Gilda snapped. "Thanks Rosie, I'm sorry. I didn't mean to call you an idiot. I'm just mad at myself."

"Well, what happened?" Rose inquired, thinking to herself that Gilda pretty much always snaps back her answers.

"Did you see that plate of doughnuts out there?" Gilda continued sputtering.

"You mean platter? Yes, I did."

"They're mine. Well, they were mine before I made my involuntary donation to this porcelain bus I'm driving at the moment."

"What? What are you talking about?" Now Rose was confused.

"I got sick to my stomach. I can't eat breads, remember?" Gilda sternly replied. "They get stuck." (Gilda tapped on the base of her neck indicating her throat.) "Right now it feels as though there's a backup of thick, yeasty bread dough all along my esophagus." Gilda sighed, "But I love doughnuts and I miss eating them. When I woke this morning, while perusing the room service menu I saw the *Morning Plate of Pastries*. Of course I looked at other menu items. I read over the details of the tropical fruit and yogurt parfait, the red potato and rosemary frittata, the egg and tomato gratin, but my eyes kept drifting back to that Morning Plate. I thought, well, doughnuts aren't exactly bread. They're usually lighter, airier and, of course sweeter. I must have set down and picked up that room service menu reading and re-reading the delightful descriptions of those doughnuts three or four times. So, after careful deliberation, I ordered the *Morning Plate of Pastries*. When room service rolled in the cart and I saw that platter of gleaming, rotund sweets, I stood in awe of how something so small could give so much. I immediately tipped the waiter, plopped down on the edge of my bed, placed the tray on my lap and proceeded to take a teeny-tiny bite out of each one. I slooowly bit into the first doughnut, savoring the essence of mapleness evenly spread along its light and airy softness. As I chewed I eyed the platter, contemplating my second bite. I went for the chocolate old-fashioned, your fav. . ."

"My favorite," Rose interrupted.

"Yes Rosie, your favorite. That one I ate a little less slowly. But I did take notice of the difference in texture between the cake doughnut and the raised doughnut. Yet both chocolate and maple icing linger on your tongue. Did you realize that, Rosie?"

"No sorry. I can't recall I've ever taken the time to make the comparison."

Gilda continued, seeming not to hear Rose. "I smiled with pleasure as the custard-filled one oozed out onto the corners of my mouth. I carefully dabbed it off so I wouldn't waste a drop, then licked my fingers. Next, I nibbled on the white and frilly-textured coconut one. I still felt okay, I made

sure to eat slowly. Next, the cinnamon and sugar doughnut holes, again, I was careful to take the smallest of bites. They were a little greasy though. But overall, the doughnuts were everything I remembered them to be."

"Were you planning to eat all of them?"

"Noo. I told you, my plan was to take just one bite of each. And that's what I did. Well almost. There were a few I couldn't get to."

"So they were just as tasty as you thought they'd be huh? Was it worth it?"

"Yes, Rosie it was. With every bite, came blissful satisfaction as I mindfully chewed, then swallowed that teeny tiny bite from each nectarean celestial sphere.

"I saw the doughnuts out there, Gilda. Those weren't exactly teeny bites."

"Well anyway, as I said, I figured one little morsel of each would satisfy my craving and wouldn't be too much for me to digest. But I started to feel full and uncomfortable so I scooted back on my bed and sipped my coffee to help wash them down a bit. It didn't take long before I got sick," Gilda spoke with despair. Her dreamy tone had changed. "So, here I am, on the floor of the bathroom. I just need to lie down for a minute."

"Okay, I'll help you. Guess it was worth it." Rose stated flatly.

"Absolutely!"

As Rose walked past the disenfranchised plate of doughnuts she threw them into the waste-basket, then set it in a corner of the room out of view. She felt badly for Gilda and could only somewhat relate to her sister's actions. Rose rarely ate doughnuts. But she could if she wanted to. If Rose was honest there had been more than a few occasions she has sat cross-legged on the floor in the quiet of any empty room she could find and meticulously taken bites out of the assorted chocolates from a box of See's Candies. These tasty excavations were always in search of her favorite guilty pleasure, the dark chocolate covered, caramel and marshmallow peccadillo. Rose knows the anxiety that comes with trekking through almost an entire box of empty calories. Yet she wouldn't end up with her head in the toilet hoping someone would show up and hold her hair. She wouldn't suffer the way Gilda just did. Rose now began to feel more sympathy than the disgust she felt when she first walked into the bathroom. She wished there was more she could do for her sister's discomfort.

Rose avoided offering to get Gilda a soda knowing it would only make matters worse. Since surgery, the bubbles of carbonated drinks cause Gilda even greater pain. So, instead Rose picked up the vanilla latte she had set down on the counter moments earlier and plopped herself into the uncomfortable, high-tech chair next to Gilda's bed, finding herself, once again, sitting quietly and watching television with her twin sister until Gilda felt better.

Sisters in Shakespeare

Born as fraternal twins, Rose and Gilda were christened with the feminine versions of their mother's favorite Shakespearian characters, Rosencrantz and Guildenstern. So it came as no surprise to those familiar with the antics of the original two scheming and jocular characters beset to fool King Hamlet that Rose and Gilda would be just as beguiling and prankish as little girls growing up in a family with a flair for the dramatic.

Throughout their childhood, these two myrmidons were inseparable, whether they were stealing their way out of trouble at school or involved in doing "makeovers" on friends who hadn't requested them but whom the twins deemed were in dire need of. Though not identical, Rose and Gilda were quite similar in appearance. Almost mirror images of one another, they were born with the same strategically placed beauty marks on their upper thighs. Rose's mark was on her right thigh; Gilda's was on the left. They also shared the ability of being able to raise only one eyebrow at a time. Rose could raise her left eyebrow; Gilda her right. When both were facing you with expressions poised in this questioning and disbelieving manner you sometimes wondered if you were indeed speaking the truth or your story was fabrication! The girls shared secrets, makeup, classroom notes and answers to exams. Once they even shared a boyfriend, though they didn't know it at the time.

The only thing these analogous sisters did not share was clothing. Their body shapes and metabolisms were very different.

Both sisters were quite pretty and active. Rose began her study of dance when she was just six years old. While in college she majored in the fine arts and graduated with a Bachelor of Arts Degree in Dance. Her size and weight had always mattered to her, though she did not openly obsess about it. Rose was naturally thin and during her years of study had devised a number of ways to maintain her "dancer's body." Some methods she used were widely popular among other dancers, gymnasts and models; some were of her own creation.

One of her more clever ideas was placing a scale on the floor directly in front of the refrigerator. Whenever she felt an urge to eat or was sincerely hungry, she was forced to step onto the scale as she approached the refrigerator. Walking around the scale or kicking it to the side would be cheating. And Rose would never cheat. If the number looking back up at her was too high or not to her liking, Rose would simply turn around and leave the kitchen without eating so much as a morsel. Besides, those were the lean years and she was too broke to have anything of real gastronomic interest in her cupboards. Her staples were warmed vegetable broth and popcorn. Years later she would come to loath them.

The contents of her refrigerator contained the other items she allowed herself to consume, such as the scant makings of lettuce sandwiches. These consisted of iceberg lettuce on a slice of whole-grain bread with a smattering of mustard (mayonnaise was too fattening). The few remaining items found in her refrigerator were usually some Suzy-Q's, and diet Dr. Pepper.

Gilda was active in her own right. She, too, attended college but had no particular major of study. Her passion was rowing. She had been involved in competitive rowing since she was twelve years of age. Like Rose, Gilda had always been popular in school but tended to show less interest in her studies than she did in boats, paddles, food and friends. During her years of study, Gilda thoroughly enjoyed her social life and indulged in super-sized helpings of nightlife, good food and good drink.

It was later, as grown women with husbands and children, when the differences in these fraternal twins became more evident. Rose managed to keep her weight down except when pregnant. Once those weeks of morning sickness passed, she allowed herself to eat anything and everything. Of course, after the baby arrived her varied systems of losing the baby fat were immediately self-enforced. The topic of such rapid and drastic weight loss was never openly discussed or addressed by her friends or family.

This was in direct contrast to the almost constant and open commentary regarding Gilda's size and weight. Years of rowing had caused Gilda to develop a strong body, with muscular arms, thick thighs and a gluteus maximus to match. And at 5'5" with no loss of interest in good food and drink, Gilda's dress size continued to increase. Though the intentions were meant to be helpful and the comments were uttered in tones of concern - "if only she would lose some of that weight" - "maybe she should consider some other exercise or sport, swimming or something, one that doesn't cause her to build so much muscle" - "she's so pretty, but . . ." it began to take a toll on Gilda.

Eventually, Gilda had begun to believe if only she did lose the weight her marriage would improve, she would get the dream job she wanted, her kids would behave, she would be happier, pretty much everything in her life would be near perfect. By the time she was in her late thirties, Gilda had had it with her weight fluctuations: up, down, up, down, up, up, down. It was during one particularly emotional phone call when Gilda told Rose she had seen a doctor about gastric surgery.

"Rosie, I found out I'm a candidate for bariatric surgery. I've thought it over. I'm going to do it. I am so sick and tired of dieting. Nothing ever works! Or, it works in the beginning but then I put all the weight back on, plus some! This is such bullshit I just can't do it anymore."

As usual, Gilda had made a decision and sounded strong in her conviction but ended her declaration in deference of her seventeen-minute older sibling with, "So Rosie, what do you think? Should I do it?"

Gastric bypass was less common at that point in time, as were the terms, "sleeve", "lap-band" and "O-ring." Rose knew very little regarding the details but had heard about some celebrity's wife recently having lap-band procedure. The outcome seemed to have worked quite well for her. She looked fabulous on every magazine cover and televised talk show.

Rose never suffered the weight gain issues her sister had, but she did have her own food demons. And while she was unable to relate to grand fluctuations on the bathroom scale, she could relate to the sadness, guilt and near self-hatred that comes with eating and then swallowing foods that seem to show up on the hips and rear ends of women of Italian/Puerto Rican descent (and the upper arms Gilda would add). After a bit of sympathetic conversation, Rose made it clear she supported her sister's decision to have the lap-band.

During the next several weeks Gilda prepared for her surgery by waiting and eating and more eating. She ate her "last" steak and garlic smashed potatoes with country gravy, her "last" hoagie and gigantic bladder-buster sized soda. Her "last" three or four servings of Rose's lavender and vanilla rice pudding (another comfort food favorite) and her "last" éclair, well, éclairs actually. Over the course of that particular day, Gilda snacked on two éclairs, one doughnut and half a cinnamon roll between meals. Two days before surgery when she and Rosie went together for her "last" hamburger fries and milkshake, Rose noticed and commented on the judgmental looks directed at them from one woman sitting at a nearby table with her toddler. This very slender and very blond woman didn't appear to have any food in front of her. As the two sisters stole glances they could see she was only picking small bites from her child's plate. They agreed, this was her normal approach to meal time. Gilda told Rose she had no use for people who looked at her with those "just-put-your-fork-down" eyes or "why don't you push yourself away from the table?" smirks. They had no idea of what her life had been like over the years, the starvation diets, counseling, fat farms, and weight-loss cruises. The money she'd spent, the constant exercise programs, and personal trainers, none seemed to yield lasting benefits. Changing the subject somewhat the sisters laughed about a recent talk show host who had gone through her day wearing a "fat suit." This was the program's focus story, testing the premise that society holds some prejudice towards and discriminates against people who are more than a little overweight and those considered medically obese.

"Big deal," Gilda scoffed. The lady who wore that suit could take the fat off at the end of the day and hang it on the back of a chair. I can't do that."

Gilda pushed what was left of her hamburger to the side, deciding she had had enough of everything that day.   Rose and Gilda firmly walked out of the fast food restaurant with Rosie shooting a sharp glare straight in the eyes of the still-staring woman.

After the surgery Rose called Gilda daily to see how her sister was recuperating. It had been only three days since the surgery and Gilda was home sounding surprisingly perky and upbeat. She responded to Rose's inquiry that day by saying, "I'm fine, a little uncomfortable, but I have a serious craving for your homemade chocolate pudding."

"I thought you could only have clear liquids for the next few days," Rose cautiously replied.

"I know," Gilda muttered with resignation in her voice.

"Well my homemade chocolate pudding is anything but clear," Rose declared almost emphatically.

"I know," Gilda retorted in a tone only the youngest child in the family (even those just minutes younger) can sustain well into adulthood, "but I reeally want some."

The soothing warmth promised by a ramekin of chocolate pudding was just the consolation Gilda felt she needed. The urge had struck her an hour ago, and she couldn't get Rosie's homemade chocolate pudding, with its earthy-dark, velvety-rich, inviting aroma out of her head. Chocolate: a food worthy of high praise and importance for centuries. While Rose was attending culinary school she had told Gilda the story of how the ancient Mayans, Incans and Aztecs had been cultivating and enjoying the fruit of the cacao tree as early as 600 AD. Gilda was sure Rose's chocolate pudding would definitely hold a place of honor in the daily diet of any ancient tribal leader. Her recipe for this fudge-like pudding invoked in Gilda's mind a dreamy solace from the sterile offerings of broth during her short hospital stay followed by her husband and kid's diligent adherence to the instruction sheet of "what to eat at home".

Nothing on that list was as appetizing or enticing as Rosie's pudding with her addition of instant espresso and pinch of chili powder and its intimate co-mingling with the Scharffenberger chocolate she insists on using. Gilda could just see the steam rising from the saucepot. She could taste the luxuriant chocolate with its smooth texture coating her tongue creating a tasty veneer over her teeth, bringing pleasure to the whole interior of her mouth. Gilda even enjoys eating the skin that forms on top of the pudding, as in her mind it only serves as edible insurance to the goodness that lies beneath.

Of course, later that afternoon Rose succumbed and lovingly prepared the pudding, then stealthily snuck two ramekins into Gilda's bedroom where she lay recuperating. Rose sat next to Gilda's bed and the two sisters spooning one of their favorite food definitions of comfort into their open and receptive mouths. Unfortunately, the silent bliss ended after only three bites. Gilda's newly constructed stomach was shocked and dismayed in sharp contrast to her taste buds. Within moments Gilda's chocolate pudding suddenly erupted back up. Rose reacted quickly grabbing the small green kidney-shaped container sitting on the nightstand designed just for matters such as this. After watching her sister frantically clean up the less-than-clear evidence and compose herself, Gilda said she would be content to simply watch Rose finish eating her chocolate decadence. But Rose could not bring herself to eat in front of her sister. Instead, she promised Gilda that she would make the pudding again at another time. The girls straightened themselves up and decided it was safer to sit and watch the Food Network together. So the sisters settled in and talked about food, kids, and husbands between Ina's whisking and rolling.

Consoling Chocolate Pudding

Ingredients:

1 14-oz can low-fat sweetened condensed milk

1 cup half and half

1/2 cup fine granulated sugar

4 ounces Scharffenberger unsweetened baking chocolate, broken into small pieces

2 tablespoons Dutch cocoa powder

1 teaspoon instant espresso powder

1/8 teaspoon chili powder

2 tablespoons cornstarch

2 large eggs plus 1 additional egg yolk

1 teaspoon vanilla extract

For garnish, if desired; 1 cup heavy cream whipped with 4 tablespoons powdered sugar

Preparation:

1) In small mixing bowl whisk together ½ the can of condensed milk, cornstarch, whole eggs and egg yolk - set aside.

2) In medium saucepot combine remaining can of condensed milk with all the half and half, sugar and cocoa powder whisking over medium heat. Continue whisking until mixture begins to simmer. Do not allow to boil.

3) Remove from heat and whisk in chocolate pieces, until melted and blended

4) Temper the egg mixture by adding one ladle of warm chocolate mixture to the egg mixture. Then add a second or third ladle of chocolate mixture to egg. Return saucepot to heat, and over low heat, slowly pour remaining egg-cornstarch mixture into warm chocolate mixture whisking constantly until well blended and mixture begins to thicken. About 5 - 7 minutes

5) Finally, remove saucepot from heat; stir in vanilla extract, espresso powder and chili powder. Ladle into individual ramekins and serve warm or chilled, if preferred.

6) Garnish with a dollop of freshly prepared whipped cream if desired.

Makes six 4-ounce servings

Rose had long quit dancing when she became pregnant with her third child and was working "as a mother and housewife" as she had come to describe herself to those who asked. But it was on a kind of dare when she decided to return to school and earn her certification as a chef just as her youngest child was finishing the second grade. Rose was following a dream she didn't even realize she had. It was while sitting on the floor lost in an array of cookbooks scattered around her. She was admiring a chef's uniform in a cooking catalog when her daughter came breezing through the living room. Sharon immediately took notice that once again her mother was entranced in a wasteland of recipe books and culinary magazines then asked the rhetorical question, "Why don't you become a chef mom?"

"I can't become a chef just like that!"

Sharon stood looking down at her mother sitting in a lotus position other women her mother's age would find uncomfortable. Rose's attention turned back down and focused on a figure in the catalog wearing black and white checkered pants beneath a crisp white bistro apron. Not really expecting an answer and without saying another word, Sharon turned on her heels and walked towards the kitchen, but not before Rose looked up and saw her daughter's raised eyebrows and pursed lips. An expression that said, fine - then don't do what you love. Nothing like the impact of a seventeen-year-old's flippant, cavalier look accompanied by an unspoken challenge to get a woman up off the floor. Rose registered in a local culinary program at the next semester.

Creating menus, adapting recipes and preparing exceptional food to please others was akin to choreographing a dance, rehearsing, and then performing in Rose's mind. Within one year of receiving her certificate, Rose was working full-time as a personal chef and culinary instructor. A rather odd dream job her sister pointed out, "Considering you don't eat."

Meanwhile Gilda was working part-time as a local news journalist and continued rowing twice a week. An avid cyclist and busy mother of two, all the exercise and insertion of the lap-band allowed her to finally lose that weight and stay fit. Gilda had learned to adapt to the restrictions of her amended stomach, some common, some unique to her. Now only able to consume four ounces at a time, Gilda's portion controls were essentially built in. And she did her best to not eat outside the band. But Gilda never really lost her interest in food or love of eating.

Rose's active involvement in the Las Vegas culinary scene introduced the twin sisters to an extensive group of friends ranging from professional chefs to waiters, bartenders, food critics and culinary retailers. Always up for any excuse to gather together for meals, Rose's invitations for volunteer guinea pigs were always accepted and looked forward to. If she went too long without hosting some kind of food gathering, open discussion ensued with expressions of disappointment among the group of friends.

It was during one of their weekly phone conversations when Gilda lightly inquired if Rose would help her host a small dinner for her daughter Megan's birthday the next week.

"Of course I will. What time?"

"Well, my house is such a disaster can we do it at your place?"

"Gilda, I don't know. How can your place be a mess? You have a housekeeper.

"I had to let her go. Every time she came through the door she made stink-face. The last time she was here I told her while she was wiping things down maybe she could wipe that look off her face. She threw down her dusting rag and walked out. So I'm between housekeepers at the moment. I can't find one to do what I need done around here."

"That's because you don't clean or pick up between visits. Your housekeepers all probably feel a sense of déjà vu. Instead of *50 First Dates* it's like *50 First Cleans*, for them, poor things. And your house is huge. Anyway, I don't know, Gilda. I'm not sure Kevin will be okay with it this time."

"Really? Why not?"

Rose began to tell her sister about her husband's recent rant. "Kevin has been acting so annoyed with me lately. All he does is moan about the cost of my cook's tools and equipment."

"Well Rosie, your kitchen has become an extension of William-Sonoma over the last three years. Your cooking is amazing, but do you really need *all* those tools? A pineapple corer, that special wooden bowl for your mezzaluna and every size strainer known to man. And how many juicers do you have now? A manual and an electric citrus juicer, not to mention those other colorful handheld juicers, a yellow for lemons, the green one for limes and the big orange one for oranges. Honestly, Rosie."

"Yes, yes I do need all those tools. At least I don't have that ridiculous tool I see everyone using these days, *the garlic press*. Gosh, use a knife!"

"That's because, for some reason, you think having hands that smell like garlic brings you closer to Nana. God rest her olive oil, garlic and *arroz con pollo* soul."

Rose continued, "I told Kevin I notice he never complains about the cost of my work while his mouth is full of the food I've cooked for him."

"Then you should try to keep his mouth constantly full." Gilda sighed, "I guess this wouldn't be the best time to ask him to let me host a party at your house. Let's wait a couple of days. He loves Megan so much though; he probably won't feel put out if it's for her."

While she and Rosie planned Megan's "Southern Belle"- themed birthday party, Gilda brought up Kevin's original concerns and agreed it really wasn't fair to expect Rose to host most every food get together for their family and friends. But the truth was Rose was the most sensitive and aware regarding Gilda's digestive limits.   A result of the doughnut disaster on board ship, the decision was made that Gilda would tend to finding seats at the dining tables and perhaps arrange them more to her liking while Rose prepared Gilda's plate of very small portions with items she knew her sister would appreciate or perhaps be interested in trying. This plan spared Gilda the temptation of over-eating then suffering the consequences for the duration of the cruise. Rose's watch-dog-like protection of her sister never waned for the remainder of the vacation or thereafter.

Of course Gilda wasn't alone in her special dietary needs. There were others among their circle of friends who had food considerations of their own. Carla, who ran her own catering business, was eating "clean" in an attempt to stay strong in her fight against cancer. Patrice was a vegan, though her husband was not, and Shelly was usually trying out the newest diet fad to lose weight. Yet Rose could always be counted on to adapt her recipes or provide alternatives when cooking to ensure everyone was well-fed and didn't feel cheated out of any aspect of enjoying a good meal. In other words, everyone always left Rose's table happy and sated.

"So Rosie, I was thinking about these dinners at your house."

"Are you bringing this up because you have another something special in mind?"

"Noo," Gilda interrupted, "well yes, I always have something special in mind, but wait, listen. I've been thinking about these dinner parties we always ask you to host and I have an idea. You and I, our family and foodie friends all love getting together for meals whether it's a special occasion or not. Actually we'll find any excuse to cook and eat together. But I realized it's so much more than

that. We don't just love eating, we love *talking* about the food. Your friend Jimmy practically gives whole sermons on dishes he's prepared. He's so passionate and informative every time he speaks on the topic of food. No matter who's sitting at your table, every one of us is on fire when the topics are recipes, chefs and restaurants. You read cookbooks as if they were the best fiction ever written, and I read diet books as if they were smut novels. And then, of course, there's the presentation of the food. Jonah and Colin certainly give you a run for your money in the table-setting and dishes department. Every gathering they attend they chant their mantra; remember, we eat with our eyes first. In spite of my O-ring, our kids' picky eating habits, your husband's body-building and high protein needs, Carla's clean eating, Shelly's diets and whoever's food allergies or intolerances, you never let that deter any one of us from enjoying every aspect of the meal you've prepared."

"Yeah, that's true," Rose replied thoughtfully. "I know I *always* do my best to balance every-one's food concerns or needs while maintaining the integrity of the dish. But I don't mind. I think of it as a challenge. I really like doing the research on what will accommodate the myriad restrictions that may find their way to my table. Gilda, when you first told me you were considering bariatric surgery, I went right out and read about what you could eat and what you had to avoid. I remember our parents weren't very excited about you having the surgery. Neither was your husband. I was the only one who originally supported your decision. And now look, turns out it was the best thing for you. You have lost a ton of weight . . . "

"A ton?!!" Gilda broke in. "I didn't need to lose a ton! Gosh Rose." Annoyed at her sister,

Gilda heard those old ghosts in her head who uttered comments about her weight all those years return in a flooded rush. *Rosie was usually more sensitive when making references to her weight,* she thought. Certainly the comment wasn't meant to be hurtful. But still, the words burned inside Gilda with the scoville units of a Ghost Pepper.

"I'm sorry, Gilda, I didn't mean it that way. You know that. I forget you still see yourself as heavy, but you're not. Think about the times I've taken you through your own closet to show you the sizes of your dresses and skirts. Feeling fat and being fat are not the same thing. The point I'm trying to make is that while the surgery addressed the size of your stomach and how much you can eat, it didn't address the matters of your head or heart in relation to food. I can remember, following your surgery it was as though you went through a kind of mourning process after your surgery. You kept talking about chewy chocolate brownies, your beloved medium-rare steaks mounted high with bleu cheese-butter and those flakey, buttery croissants we ate when we went to Paris that one year."

"I did, didn't I? And you were such a snob when we got back to the States. You wouldn't even allow American-baked croissants anywhere near your lips. You said they tasted like parchment paper."

"That's because they did."

"Well, you didn't have to say out it loud while we were standing in the middle of the coffee shop.

"Hey, do you remember when we were kids and our entire family went to Nana and Bubba's house every year for Thanksgiving? Bubba would tear off a piece of fresh sourdough bread - it was so crispy and crunchy on the outside but soft and chewy on the inside. Then he would use that big hunting knife he always wore in the sheath on his belt buckle, cut off a chunk of sharp cheddar cheese and Italian *salumi*. I never understood why he wore that knife. Was it just for cutting up food or what? Anyway, he would slap the cheese and *salumi* onto the hunk of bread, then ceremoniously hand one to each of us five grandchildren. God, I'm making myself drool."

"Yup, I remember, answered Rose. So good. This is exactly what I'm talking about. The more I learn about bariatric surgery the more I realize the amended stomach doesn't have any recollection or emotional attachment to food memories, dinners out, food gifts or any of the other components that come with the joy of eating." Rose was contemplative as she spoke.

"Oh Rosie, that's so true. Every time I go in to have my band inflated, absolutely it's helping me maintain a healthy weight. But it has no idea how much I enjoy thinking and pondering at ten a.m. what I'm going to order at eight p.m. My stomach doesn't know the delectable decision I have to make between avocado egg rolls or pulled pork sliders when we go watch games at Kevin's favorite sports bar. Hey, I'm realizing Kevin never complains about the cost of those beers and all that food when we go watch those games!"

Once again ignoring her sister's comment about her husband, Rose chimed in. "What about those times when we come home from work after a long day that started with a difficult morning of harsh words? You come home, walk into the dining room and see the table set with a meal that says "I'm sorry." Such a simple gesture, yet so meaningful. Even though he can't really cook, I love it when Kevin does that for me."

"He does that for you?" Gilda asked incredulously. "Vince never does that for me. See Rose, our love of food isn't *just* the eating. It's everything associated with the food. Seriously, since I can only eat about four ounces at a time now, what I do choose *really* matters. And since most of our friends are as choosy about what they put into their bodies and as passionate about the whole food experience as we are, I was thinking, we should start a supper club."

"A supper club?" asked Rose, now intrigued.

"Yeah, each month one of us will take a turn hosting the dinner. The host or hostess for that month will choose the food theme and then we all prepare a dish in conjunction with that theme. It'll be a potluck, then no one person is responsible for incurring the entire cost of the meal or having to do all the work by themselves. Maybe we could bring copies of our recipes to share with one another. So what do you think?" Gilda smiled.

Their reminiscent jaunt down this epicurean lane left both sisters feeling hungry. Standing in their respective kitchens, refrigerator doors open, Gilda's presentation of her idea inspired them both to grab a snack. Gilda cut out a chunk of Megan's leftover birthday cake, Rose chose an apple. Rose continued listening to her sister as she pulled the apple slicer from a drawer laden with tools and cut the apple into perfect wedges then proceeded to scoop small mounds of almond butter onto her apple slices. "I think it's a great idea Gilda." Rose mumbled as she munched away at her apple. Gilda could hear the crunch, crunch, crunch, of something coming through her ear piece, causing her to rethink her selection.

"What are you eating?"

"An apple. A supper club would give me the opportunity to try out new recipes, re-mix old ones and experiment with original creations before preparing them for my clients or teaching. Actually, this is such a good idea, Gilda I'm going to prepare something very special for you for dinner tonight. How 'bout you come over and I'll make my garden gazpacho to ease this summer heat? And I'll make some white sangria to go with it."

"This is why I love my twin. You can always read my mind. That's *just* what I was craving!" exclaimed Gilda. Tossing the remains of her cake into the open, over-flowing trash can, Gilda called out to her husband that she was heading over to her sister's for dinner. He and the kids would be on their own.

Garden Gazpacho

Ingredients:

4 ripe beef steak or 6 ripe Roma tomatoes - peeled, seeded and chopped*

3 green onions - chopped

2 stalks celery - chopped

1 English or Hothouse cucumber - peeled and small diced

3 fresh carrots - shredded with a peeler

3 cloves fresh garlic - minced

3 tablespoons rice wine vinegar

2 tablespoons extra virgin olive oil

1 cup vegetable stock

1 cup vegetable juice

1/2 cup water

2 tablespoons fresh basil - *chiffonade*

Salt and pepper to taste

 *Note: To peel and seed tomatoes, using a paring knife, simply score a small X at the top end of each tomato and place in a pot of gently boiling water for about 30 seconds. Using a slotted spoon, remove tomatoes from the water and when cool enough to handle peel off the skin with your hands. Cut each tomato in half to spoon out the seeds, than cut according to recipe dimensions. This process is known as *tomato concasse*.

Garnishes: 1 avocado-diced, 2 fresh limes-quartered, roasted-salted sunflower seeds, buttered croutons.

Preparation:

1) In a very large glass or other non-reactive mixing bowl combine all ingredients from tomatoes to salt and pepper. Cover and refrigerate for at least 2 hours.

2) Serve in individual bowls - top each with suggested garnishes.

Makes six 4-ounce servings

Rose and Gilda shared the idea of a supper club among a select group of friends. It was met with great enthusiasm by each. However, it took some time before the first gathering of the Friends Amid Food commenced. Actually it wasn't until summer began to come to a close and the two sisters had returned from their vacation when it finally happened.

Caribbean Breezes in Las Vegas - October

It was late afternoon on the first Friday of the month. Rose and Gilda still wore rich shades of cocoa-brown on their tanned skin, while adhering to the relaxed demeanor well practiced during their three-week Caribbean cruise. Gilda had taken lots of pictures which gave her detailed references to follow for her project in re-creating the style and decor for the tablescape she had decided to assemble. The pictures in both Rose and Gilda's minds were unsullied. This meant the presentation and the foods for their first supper club would be as close to authentic Caribbean as possible in Las Vegas.

The weather was cooperating as the sun was streaming in through Rose's plantation shutters. A slight breeze wound its way through her kitchen, teasing her neighbors, carrying the scent of her Cinnamon Chicken and Plantains cooking on the stove. Rose was anxious to see what the other friends would bring to dinner, hoping they would stick to her dinner theme, engaging the concept of the simplicity and satisfying cuisine she and her sister had discovered in Barbados, Martinique, St. Kitts and Grenada.

Rose was dressed in her long, white bistro apron, hair pulled up and back in a loose chignon, the same style she has been wearing since her ballerina days, while wistfully humming a mindless tune as she cooked. With speed, grace and intention, she added pinches of salt and shakes of cinnamon, then called Gilda over to sample a few tastes and give her honest critiques.

Between tastes Gilda bustled back and forth from her car to the dining room, putting the finishing touches on her colorful tablescape. She has a recognized gift for setting the tone and atmosphere for any type of gathering. She continued to busy herself transforming Rose's patio and dining room with twinkling lights. Tissue paper palm trees and oversized flowers smiled with the colors of the Caribbean, varying shades of blue ranging from deep ocean to light, wispy sky. Bright yellows lay comfortably warm against soft, pastel yellows. Effervescent greens mixed with mint greens and lavender. Gilda had already set the table with multicolored plates, bowls and cups to imitate the vibrant architecture she so loved in Nassau. Butterfly napkin rings hugged the mismatched, floral patterned linens that lay atop each plate awaiting their own transformation from still accents to useful open-winged tools for the meal.

In truth, neither Rose nor Gilda really needed to refer to the photos of their trip. The taste of the spices, the warmth of the rum and the images of the islands were as fresh in their minds as the Mahi Mahi Colin had promised to bring to dinner.

When the sisters finished their chosen tasks, they took a moment to sit outside on the now beach-like patio, ready and waiting for the Friends Amid Food to arrive. Gilda chatted on about who was coming to dinner while Rose nodded slowly, sipping the Goombay Smash rum drink Gilda prepared for her. While on vacation Rose had referred to these as her "morning smoothies," making no apologies for her early imbibing.

Their brief period of rest came to an end with a cringe at the slamming of the sliding pocket screen door no one seemed to be able to open or close properly, including Maureen who was the first of the Friends to arrive. She entered smiling sheepishly at her noisy entrance, cradling a lovely Key Lime pie in both hands and bottle of wine tucked under her left arm. Maureen was almost immediately followed by Carla who walked in with a fabulous looking orange and yellow tart sure to complement Maureen's dessert. By six-thirty Rose's open, airy home was filled with Friends, food and conversation.

The calypso music clamored in the background, as the pitcher of Goombay Smashes made its way among the guests. Carla was now embroiled in her battle against melanoma. Always mindful of what she ate and drank, she never allowed those restrictions to keep her from enjoying all that life with her foodie Friends had to offer. But she did remain faithful to clean eating. Instead of the Goombay Smash, she came prepared with her own concoction of an organic and sugar-free cocktail. She used a mixture of top shelf vodka mixed in agave syrup and a solution of organic pomegranate and blueberry juices. She never permitted sugar substitutes to pass through her lips, claiming they had originally been designed as bug repellants. Carla offered to share her potion with the others, explaining why her cocktail was actually good for them! Patrice was game and happily accepted Carla's gracious offer.

Before Carla began to feel the effects soon to be induced by her healthy cocktail, she set about serving up her appetizer of Black Bean Salsa with Exotic Fruit with her Homemade Plantain Chips. Carla detailed the preparation of her appetizer between sips.

"Wow! Carla, this is a wonderful game of south chasing further south. I love how the warm plantains complement the fruit dip," exclaimed Gilda as she held two chips in her hand. Carla's fruit dip was a perfumed mixture of earthy black beans and sensuous, juicy, exotic fruits. She told the group how she created a blend of mango, papaya, avocado, plum tomatoes, garlic, jalapeno, and cilantro then pulled the flavors together with freshly minced garlic and lime juice.

"Gilda's right about this taste combination. There is definitely something grand going on in my mouth right now. This fruit salsa is a veritable parade of tastes, Carla," Maureen announced.

When the Friends felt they had sufficiently caught up on what was new with everyone, Gilda proclaimed it was time to address the matter at hand: dinner.

"I think it would be nice if we all gathered around the table and did an introduction of our contributions to the meal. Tell us if you've prepared an original recipe, an old family favorite or whatever. We can do this at every supper club meeting; make it a standard thing. What do you think?" Rose suggested.

"Excellent idea, Rose," agreed Jonah. "Colin and I brought copies of our recipes in case anyone wanted one."

So the tradition was instilled each Friend, glass of wine or other libation in hand, would gather around the dining table to introduce their contribution to the dining table. Describing the dish, its

origins, the ingredients used, where they found those ingredients (Jimmy was already notorious for using ingredients found only in offbeat locations) and how it was prepared. The evening's food stories had all the members giddy with excitement about taking the first bite of every dish. When all the food introductions were complete, Gilda turned the calypso music up and the eating began.

Rose's face wore the smile of satisfaction that comes with choosing the perfect gift for a dear friend, as she watched each supper club member plate up and yum on about her Cinnamon Chicken and

Plantains.

"Who would have thought that cinnamon and chicken would go so well together?" Sophie asked.

Rose shared she had followed the recipe just as it was taught to her while she and Gilda were visiting the island of St. Kitts. The teachers at the Caribbean Cooks Cooking School were sisters as well. The eldest sister was a food historian, so her cooking demonstration was layered with historical facts and trivia about the food and the islands. This made the class even more interesting for seasoned cooks and novices.

"Although, we thought we might have to say this dish was faux Caribbean, since the sisters who own the school and taught the class were white as the picket fence outside their little school and as American as Wonder Bread. Turns out they were from the state of Washington!" Gilda explained as she worked her way around the room refilling glasses. She had decided to wait a bit before eating anything more. The options displayed on her sister's table were abundant, but she knew she had to choose wisely. Even after making her rounds with the pitcher she still couldn't decide.

The origins of the teachers for this dish didn't seem to matter. Rose and Gilda watched as their guests allowed the taste of this ultra-moist, slow cooked chicken and onions in a rich broth containing butter, cinnamon and brown sugar to slide down their throats. The round slices of soft-cooked plantains added texture and served to offset the sweetness of the cinnamon and sugar. Rose had prepared a small, specialized portion of her entrée for Patrice and Carla, substituting firm tofu for the chicken and using vegetable broth. Both women were, of course, grateful.

Sophie and Kyle were the youngest members of the supper club, but age was no deterrent to their culinary curiosity, experience and contribution. This young couple impressed their fellow foodies at this first official gathering of the Friends Amid Food. Upon their arrival, each walked in carrying one large and heavy vessel. Sophie carried a rice cooker filled with warm, white basmati rice and pigeon peas. Kyle carried the heavier slow-cooker bubbling with Jamaican Brown Chicken Stew.

They alternately spoke, explaining the preparation of their dish which began in a manner similar to Rose's Cinnamon Chicken and Plantains. It is step three when this copiously flavored dish takes its own turn by incorporating a fusion of seasonings. Garlic, curry, thyme, allspice and red pepper flakes come together in a broth of red wine, diced tomatoes and black beans. Like their own union, this was a marriage of earth and sky, spice (Kyle) and sweet (Sophie). This robust mixture is then poured over the virgin steamed basmati and pigeon peas. Everyone agreed, as they consumed the Jamaican Brown Chicken Stew, this was not their grandmother's stew.

These two succulent chicken entrees were catapulted into an even higher harmonious state when accompanied by Jonah and Colin's Caribbean Seafood Salad and the Bahamian Shrimp and Scallops Salad. The Caribbean Seafood Salad was a superb mesh of tastes that was a true illustration of all the Caribbean has to offer: fresh seafood entwined with the tartness of citrus and perfectly balanced with the best that the bluest of oceans. Meaty cubes of fresh Mahi Mahi along with strips of Tilapia were massaged with a light coating of mayonnaise, Dijon mustard, white wine, dried ginger and a pinch of salt. Then the fleshy and delicate white fish were ever-so-slightly broiled, just enough to properly cook them, yet maintain their characteristic clean linen-white look. No additional seasonings were added directly to the Mahi Mahi or the Tilapia. Colin explained this was done to avoid any distractions from the taste of the coating which also serves to preserve the moistness of the fish. Lump crabmeat is added for sweetness. The remaining mixture of mayonnaise, mustard and ginger are combined with freshly diced tomato, cucumber and the addition of a secret ingredient the boys refused to share. Then, using the most important and affordable of culinary tools in food preparation , his hands, Jonah demonstrated in the air how he had gently combined the plump white fish in with the remaining dressing. Colin had arranged the seafood on a bed of romaine garnished with rings of red onion. Slices of fresh mango and avocado were interspersed along leaves of endive set in the   upright position.

"The endive serves the dual purpose of food and tool since you use the leaves as spoons to scoop up this delectable salad," Jonah declared as Colin demonstrated.

Jonah's Bahamian Shrimp and Scallops exemplified the notion of eating food with our eyes before actually spooning it into our mouths. Sweet baby shrimp and bay scallops were poached for only five minutes then joined by a party of diced red onion, celery, red and orange bell peppers, cucumber, tomatoes, freshly squeezed lime juice, Worcestershire sauce and just a dash of red hot sauce. What a rainbow of colors and tastes! If food could be a melody, then this salad was a song. If flavors could dance on your tongue, then this salad extended a waltz across the palate.

Jonah told the attentive listeners how he first folded together the poached shrimp, scallops and onion in a huge bowl. The mixture was placed in the refrigerator for about one hour and then the remaining food spectrum of colors are added.

"I gotta tell you," Colin chimed in, "this salad tastes even better the next day as that just gives time for the sweetness of the vegetables and the spice of the dressing to joyfully cozy up into a kind of quiet, slow dance with the shellfish, they have likely been eyeing all night from the other side of the bowl."

"Okay, that's it, I've made my choice." Gilda laughed. "I'll have two ounces of the Bahamian Shrimp and Scallops and two ounces of your Caribbean Seafood Salad guys. They look great and you made them sound utterly delicious."

Dessert was all about fruit, of course. There was a fruit salad, prepared by Jimmy with a healthy and unexpected kick thanks to the addition of the matador of all tequilas, Patron. At his urging, everyone "kicked" off dessert with a few shots of it just for good measure. By this time Carla was almost slurring on about the healthful benefits of clean, clear alcoholic beverages as she slammed her shot glass down on the table. The fruit salad, most appreciated by Patrice, was very simple, a combination of freshly cut pineapple, mangos, papayas and kiwi. Then the fruit was bathed in a simple syrup infused with fresh lime juice, brown sugar and more Patron. Zests of lime was caringly scattered like fairy dust over the top, embellishing the fruit.

The fruit bowl segued nicely into the Key Lime pie prepared by Maureen. Maureen is the supper club's research and resource member. There isn't an espresso machine or cook's knife she isn't knowledgeable about. Her favorite culinary reads are, *Cooks Illustrated* and *Cuisine at Home*. Her Key Lime pie was a perfect rendition of the recipe from Cooks. The pie filling was a rich-light, custard of the juice and zest from real Key Limes. Maureen explained, for those who were not aware, that Key Limes are packed with a sweet-tart punch and are more yellowish in color than green.

"Did you all know limes are incredibly high in vitamin C? The British used to make sure their ships were well stocked with plenty of limes for their sailors to stave off scurvy. Just goes to show, good things really do come in small packages," Maureen stated with the confidence of referenced knowledge.

The freshly-squeezed lime juice is then vigorously whisked together with egg yolks and sweetened condensed milk. The mixture is carefully poured into a standard graham cracker crust. Maureen topped her pie with piped homemade whipped cream, "whipped with my new copper whisk," she interjected, and ultra-thin slices of more Key Limes. Her pie was concurrently sweet, tangy and refreshing.

Carla's Mango Tart, a bright, yet soft, yellow-orange color was a lovely and placid partner sitting next to the bright green of the Key Lime. You could almost see a gentle Caribbean breeze swaying its way across the table of these fruit-based desserts. Truly, this array of desserts echoed the landscape of the Caribbean as Rose and Gilda remembered it.

Carla's tart, she told the Friends, was also derived directly from a recipe she uncovered years ago and chose not to stray from. Beginning with a traditional pastry crust filled with a lime based cream, an affluent mix of whole milk, egg yolks, sugar, cornstarch, butter and Persian Lime zest but not the juice. The dense custard is then topped with slices of fresh mango that curve around and around, creating a concentric pinwheel pinned in the center with fresh kiwi.

Although it was only Rose and Gilda who wore the tanned skin, every member of the supper club felt as though they, too, had just returned from the Caribbean. At the end of this evening meal, each partaker wore the same relaxed and satisfied smile of those fortunate souls who lie soaking up the warmth of the sun and enjoy the tickling of cool ocean breezes on all their senses. As these Friends Amid Food moved their party out to the tropic-decorated patio, they pictured themselves reclining on lounges or hammocks on white sandy beaches inhaling the scents of fresh seafood mixed with the occasional hint of dark rum. It was the fabulous food experience that carried these Friends to this dreamy destination.

Blackbean Salsa with Exotic Fruit

Ingredients:

1 (15-oz) can black beans - drained and rinsed

1 large ripe plum tomato - peeled, seeded and chopped

1 large avocado - peeled and diced

1 fresh papaya - peeled, seeded and diced

1 fresh mango - peeled, seeded and diced

1 jalapeno pepper - seeded and finely chopped - be sure to wear gloves

1 large clove of garlic-minced

Freshly squeezed juice of one lime

1 tablespoon chopped fresh cilantro

Kosher salt to taste

For Chips: 3 - 4 plantains and light canola oil for frying

Preparation:

1) Combine all ingredients through the lime juice in large serving bowl. Season to taste with salt. Gently stir in chopped cilantro. Cover and refrigerate until ready to use.

2) For plantain chips: peel each plantain and slice into 1-inch rounds. Heat oil in skillet and using slotted spoon, carefully spoon about 1/3 of sliced plantains into hot oil. You will probably need to do this in 3-4 batches depending upon size of your skillet. Do not overcrowd skillet. When plantains are lightly browned on one side gently turn over and brown other side. Immediately place browned plantains onto dish lined with a paper towel and lightly season with salt.

Makes four 4-ounce servings

Cinnamon Chicken and Plantains

Ingredients

1 tablespoon olive oil and 1 tablespoon bacon fat

1 large Spanish onion, chopped

1/4 cup unsalted butter

8 chicken thighs, bone-in but skin removed

1 tablespoon cinnamon

1½ cups low-sodium chicken or vegetable broth

2 tablespoons dark brown sugar

2-3 ripe plantains - thinly sliced in rounds

1/2 cup dark raisins

Salt and pepper to taste

Preparation: Preheat oven to 375 degrees

1) In a large oven-proof, heavy Dutch oven heat oil, bacon fat and butter until butter is melted.

2) Sauté chopped onions until soft and translucent

3) Season chicken thighs with salt and pepper, add to onion mixture and cook until browned

4) Pour in chicken broth, adding cinnamon

5) Bring entire mixture to a gentle boil, reduce heat and simmer covered for about 20 minutes.

6) Using a sharp knife, carefully remove peels from plantains. Slice each plantain into 1/2 inch rounds (rotelles).

7) Stir in brown sugar, raisins and sliced plantains, cooking mixture another 7-10 minutes, stirring occasionally. Plantains should turn a brighter shade of yellow.

8) Remove Dutch oven from the stove and place in pre-heated oven, covered, until chicken is cooked through and fork tender. About 20-30 minutes

Makes eight 4-ounce servings

Caribbean Seafood Salad

Ingredients:

1 cup good quality mayonnaise

1 tablespoon good dry white wine (one you would drink)

1/2 teaspoon kosher salt

8 plum tomatoes - diced

1 cup diced cucumber - English (also known as Hot House)

1/2 teaspoon Old Bay seafood seasoning

1/4 teaspoon ground white pepper

1 cup low-sodium vegetable stock + water

1/2 lb. fresh Mahi Mahi plus ½ lb. Halibut, Haddock, Rockfish or other meaty white fish - poached

1 tablespoon Dijon mustard

1 teaspoon cinnamon

8 ounces crab meat

Romaine lettuce leaves - rinsed

Pinch of sugar

Salt and pepper to taste

Unsalted butter for greasing pan

Garnishes: sliced avocados, red onion and mango

Preparation:

1) Lightly butter a large skillet or 9 x 13-inch pan with unsalted butter. Season Mahi Mahi and Halibut (or white fish of your choice) with salt and pepper. Place fish in skillet or pan and pour enough water to cover fish and simmer for 7-10 minutes, until fish is done and flakey. Remove fish from poaching liquid and set aside until ready to use.

2) In medium mixing bowl whisk together mayonnaise, mustard, wine, cinnamon, salt and sugar until well incorporated. Cover bowl with plastic wrap and refrigerate about 1 hour.

3) When mayonnaise mixture is ready, in a separate large mixing bowl, gently combine crabmeat, tomatoes, cucumber, Old Bay seasoning and white pepper.

4) Gently fold mayonnaise mixture into seafood mixture.

5) Tear off clean and dried romaine lettuce leaves, placing either one leaf on each individual plate or create a "bed" of several leaves on a large platter. Scoop mounds of crabmeat onto lettuce leaves. Garnish with the slices of avocado, onion and mango.

Makes eight 4-ounce servings

Mango Tart

Ingredients for Crust:

1¼ cups all-purpose flour

8 tablespoons cold unsalted butter - cut into cubes

3 tablespoons ice water - more if needed

1/4 cup powdered sugar

1/4 teaspoon salt

Ingredients for Filling:

1 cup whole milk

3 large egg yolks

1/3 cup fine granulated sugar, (also known as Baker's sugar)

2 tablespoons cornstarch

2 tablespoons unsalted butter

2 teaspoons lime zest

Ingredients for Topping:

2 fresh mangos - peeled and thinly sliced

1 kiwifruit - peeled and sliced

Note: You will need a tart pan with a removable bottom

Preparation: Preheat oven to 400 degrees

1) Prepare crust in food processor by combining flour, powdered sugar and salt, pulsing until blended. Add butter and pulse again until mixture looks like coarse cornmeal. Add ice water one tablespoon at a time, pulsing until mixture comes together into a ball.

2) Remove dough from bowl and flatten into a thick disk. Wrap in plastic wrap and refrigerate until firm, about 1 hour.

3) On lightly floured surface, roll out dough into 11" round. Transfer dough to 9"x1" round tart pan. Trim dough even with rim of pan. Return to refrigerator another 10 minutes.

4) Line tart pan with beans or pie weights and bake for 20 minutes, remove beans or pie weights and bake another 15 minutes until crust is a light golden brown.

While crust is baking:

1) Prepare lime filling, using a 2-quart saucepot, heat milk to simmering. In small mixing bowl, whisk together yolks and baker's sugar until blended. Whisk in cornstarch until mixture is smooth.

2) Continue whisking while slowly adding half the warm milk mixture.

3) Pour egg-yolk mixture into saucepot with remaining milk, whisking constantly to avoid lumps.

4) Continue cooking until mixture comes to boil and thickens, about 2 minutes.

5) Remove pot from heat and stir in butter and lime zest.

6) Pour cream filling mixture into a small bowl, cover with plastic wrap and refrigerate about 1 hour.

7) Spoon filling mixture into baked/cooled tart crust.

8) Arrange mango slices and kiwifruit on top of tart filling.

9) Loosen sides of pan from tart and place pan base with tart on large cake or other serving plate.

Makes ten 4-ounce servings

The Potato - Autumn in Tuscany - November

I'm a potato - a potato with aspirations. As I bump and tumble around in this crate, I can see, through the holes of my box, thin rays of light peering in along the hinges of the semi-truck that carries me and the others to our various destinations. My fellow spuds and I all aspire to something

different, but of course we are unable to communicate these unique visions for ourselves to one another directly. We are, after all, potatoes, so while we have eyes, we don't have ears to hear or mouths to speak of our hopes and dreams. But we do have hopes and dreams. And at times, we can discern ways to communicate them to one another.

While I'm not absolutely sure, there was some murmuring that the potato that bumps along beside me has visions of becoming a work of art. Yes, a work of art to be viewed, not eaten. A Mr. Potato Head they say! I've only heard about them. But to me they seem to be a ridiculous, therapy-ready display of a once natural masterpiece of starchy potassium, and complex carbohydrates, not to mention vitamins C and B6. But really, Mr. Potato Head? What a commercial sell out of an existence! For me, being poked and pinned with toothpicks and having raisins substituted for my eyes, a baby carrot for my nose, parsnips for arms, and arugula hair is not exactly my idea of greatness. On the other hand, if you truly enjoy the contemporary arts and spending time with children, I suppose the idea is more appealing.

There may be a few potato comrades below me who envision themselves swimming in pools of cheese, heavy cream and unsalted butter seasoned only with kosher salt and fresh-cracked pepper and then emerging as a rich au gratin. I would consider that a kind of "ugly duckling" transformation. Yes, that is a worthy end, if one is a Yukon Gold. Those succulent tubers eager to become a side dish with class and show-stopping looks, when prepared properly, are to be commended.

There are some adventurers among us who look forward to the prospect of being transformed through massage. I'm talking deep-tissue massage with a top-shelf olive oil, skins on, of course, during the massage. Believe it or not, many of us potato tubers are rather modest. As members of the nightshade family and years of being considered inedible and poisonous, it has taken us a very long time to rebuild our self-esteem. Thank goodness for Sir Walter Raleigh and his hunches.

After a good massage, my brothers will be roasted to enhance their natural earthy flavor, then introduced and blended with garlic from California - Gilroy California. The garlic, too, is roasted sweet and brown. Then our relaxed and receptive potatoes along with the sweet, medicinal sister of the lily (garlic) will come together to create the ever-popular garlic-roasted smashed potatoes. Those spuds and their willingness to mix with those crazy Californians is admirable.

On the less-than-admirable side are those who seek, in my opinion, a more mediocre outcome, that of the fast-food French fry. Stripped and cut in military uniformity, all to the same size, same shape, same width, then submerged in a bubbling hot bath of oil. Oh my! I've even heard that the oil is not always of good quality nor is it always clean. The finish? Salt, salt, salt, often followed by a near drowning in acidic catsup, and in some cases, even worse, commercially-prepared mayonnaise. What is the point? I suppose for those spuds, it is the never waning popularity of French fries and burgers or fish and chips. Likely it is just the fame of the pommes frites they find so alluring. We come from good soil, good farming practices. We come from Idaho! Why do that to yourself? Some consider hash browns and tater tots to be perhaps a small step up from that end. I'm not sure I agree. I won't even go into potato chips. There isn't one of us here who actively seeks that role.

Earlier this morning as we were all being loaded onto the truck, my eyes saw the fingerlings piled onto the other side of the semi. We all know most of them hope to be directed to a life of being drizzled with high quality olive oil, then hand turned with sea salt and Herbs de Provence. From there they are laid out in a single layer onto a pan, All-Clad if they're lucky, and are roasted and toasted to a state of crispy perfection, their natural hues of purples, reds and browns only highlighted by the rubdown of oil and herbs that are now cooked into their skins. I almost feel tempted to join them. A wonderfully simple example of top-shelf taste.

But my aspirations extend beyond that. It may be a quixotic hope, but it is my dream to be treated to a process that requires patient fortitude and true culinary acumen. It is my dream to culminate with a finish that only those who appreciate the balance of taste and texture and the technique of trained hands can understand. I aspire to become . . . gnocchi.

It is to the dedicated cook that I desire to give of myself. Like those who comprise the supper club known as Friends Amid Food. Is it an urban legend? I don't really know for sure. But if it is true, if this supper club, Friends Amid Food, really exists, that is where I yearn to go.

The story that quietly stirs among the spuds is that of a dinner held in Las Vegas Nevada, one cool November evening. It has been said it was one the paramount meals offered by the Friends to one another. The theme was "Italian Foods of Autumn-Small Bites With Big Taste." The evening offered an array of appetizers, each producing a blend of flavors true to the season, thereby bringing the visual beauty that is autumn to the palatable enjoyment of each member in attendance.

The hosts on that particular evening were members Colin and Jonah. This couple is known for their creative originality and attention to detail. These two men work together in such harmony, reading one another's thoughts, finishing one another's sentences, and on many occasions eating off of one another's plates. They are mystically in tune in all their joint ingenious endeavors. Their cooperative efforts bring about displays generally only seen in designer magazines, and of course, can be seen in the small, well-stocked culinary shop they own. Colin and Jonah together share in every aspect of managing the store. Colin's forte is the styling of the vignettes and displays, while Jonah tends to the balancing of company finances.

It was their specialized and original invitation that set the tone for future invitations. No, they were not satisfied to only email the food theme, date and time as others had done before them. Instead they projected photographic scenes of autumn in Italy on a kind of bulletin board e-message. Interspersed were pictures of comfort and rustic foods all displayed in a manner of gourmand. The other supper club members were most inspired by this invitation.

The first of the Friends to arrive that evening they say was Diana. She showed up with her

renowned onion tart. The onions were caramelized to a darkened, sweet perfection and baked upon a crust so buttery and light Jacques Pepin would have been humbled. It was flawless. Colin offered slices of baguette topped with a fig and roasted hazelnut jam. Atop the sweet crunchy jam were perched ever-so-thin slices of pippin apples and a final sprinkling of pecorino cheese. It has been said that the woman who championed this supper club, Gilda, has a love affair with butter that borders on the obscene, but when she took her teeny-tiny bite of this grouping of flavors atop a small slice of bread without butter, she garbled something about how once again Colin's butter-less offering to supper club was awe-inspiring.

But there was more at this festival of flavors. Jonah's acorn squash was roasted soft and sweet with brown sugar and maple syrup, a traditional East Coast autumn treat. In addition, Jonah prepared his family's recipe of turkey and zucchini meatloaf baked with an apricot glaze. To maintain their theme of small bites, Jonah prepared the meatloaf in individual fluted rounds, one for each Friend to enjoy on his or her own. As the centerpiece around which to set the dishes Gilda's sister, Rose, prepared a soup. Hers was a seasonally creative rendition of bouillabaisse. While she did include the traditional ingredients of seafood, tomatoes, onion, wine, saffron and herbs, she kept the seafood to a minimum only halibut, clams and red snapper - while premiering cubes of roasted, seasoned pumpkin. Delicious. The ongoing jovial conversations came to a noticeable halt. Only quiet murmurings of "mmmm" and "oooh" could be heard around the small apartment as the Friends began to indulge in the cornucopia of flavors.

There were desserts, of course. Colin prepared small squares of pumpkin cake that contained nothing other than the essence of pumpkin and complementary spices. Uncomplicated, straight forward and moist. Maureen prepared an autumn staple, apple crisp. Hers was one of which the other Friends claimed they had never tasted. Maureen explained she used her mini food processor to grind the steel cut oats, creating a healthier and tastier topping. Her efforts gave complexity and interest to what can sometimes be an oatmeal mush of a topping. Though I am a potato, I know my produce and have learned that each of the thousands of apple varieties available have their own specialties in recipes. For example, golden delicious are best suited for applesauce, pippin for pies and gala for the lunch box. Maureen told the Friends she used a combination of three varieties, giving her apple crisp an intertwining of taste enhanced by her crisp-sweet topping. It is rumored that the Friends each took some to their respective homes and enjoyed left over apple crisp for breakfast for as many mornings as they could make it last.

But I allow myself to become distracted by this menu and its bounty. I return now to my visions of those spuds lucky enough to be transformed into - gnocchi. Even this Italian word when translated is one I can relate to. It literally means. . . "lumps." I just happen to be covered in lumps and divots in my natural state. This seems just another sign of my desired destiny. It was supper club member Michael who prepared the dish I aspire to become.

Gnocchi is a laborious, multi-faceted task of love, endurance, dexterity and the right kitchen tools and equipment. Michael possessed all of these things. On that Sunday morning, he began by gathering my relatives, Yukon Golds, who were picked, packed, sold and bought. He first washed them clean. Aaaaahhh, a bath; I can just see it! Remember, we have never been washed, only brushed off maybe. Michael quickly and efficiently peeled the skins from those fortunate next of kin, placed them in a large saucepot of cold, salted water and cooked them until soft. The starchy water was drained, with a small amount saved, and my predecessors were put through his food mill until they were light and fluffy. Seasonings were next - quality salt, white pepper, freshly grated nutmeg some flour, oil and eggs. This combination came together naturally, as if by instinct. The now potato dough (take that pâte à choux!) was ready to be kneaded and massaged, a stress-releasing fourteen strokes of heaven at his hands. Then Michael shaped the now soft dough into a chubby loaf. From there, he cut a section of dough off, rolled it into a cord like shape that was 3/8 inches thick and 1 1/2 inches in length.

Next came the artistry that required Michael's famed patience and willingness to engage. While not all cooks own one and must instead, use the common fork, Michael had in his culinary tool arsenal, the much-coveted gnocchi board. There are some who are adventurous enough to try their hand at making gnocchi, but use a kitchen fork rather than attempt to use the board. Michael had, of course, purchased this mighty little tool at Colin and Jonah's culinary shop. Michael's well stocked kitchen rivaled even Rose's since he worked part time at their shop. He did a little bit of everything, sales, shipments, receiving. He was also the shop's favored gift-wrap-girl, since his flair for style was indisputable. Michael lightly floured the board, took one precise section he cut from the pastry cord, and with the gentleness one might use when handling a hummingbird caught mid-flight, rolled the little potato puff along the gnocchi board creating small grooves which would be embracing his long-awaited sage-butter sauce. Each piece of dough watched excitedly as the puff that went before him was rolled and placed to the side. I can only imagine the excitement!

When Michael had finished, his partner John came into the kitchen to see a collection of puffy white clouds lined up and ready to be eased into a pot of gently boiling water. They were allowed to go in just a few at a time. No overcrowding, no fighting for space, just those puffs milling around as if on a raft floating down the lazy river ride at the water park. And not too long either Michael reached for another favored tool known as a spider to gingerly remove the gnocchi after just one minute or so. The cooked gnocchi were lightly drizzled with browned unsalted butter and waited calmly while Michael went on to prepare his light butternut squash sauce. There was joy all around. They say his sauce was simple, consisting of unsalted, browned butter, fresh sage and a bit of salt.

When it was time, all the gnocchi were placed into a bowl of the prepared sauce in which they could roll and loll, allowing the sauce to seep into their individual grooves. If only I were there.

While dining that evening, John told the other Friends that Michael had spent the entire day in the kitchen doting over his preparation of the gnocchi.   Michael nodded his head in quiet pride and agreement while sipping his proverbial martini, green apple for the season. (Martinis were evidently Michael's before-dinner beverage of choice.) Michael's time, patience and efforts were rewarded with the accolades of appreciation by his fellow supper club members.

I recently heard that Michael has since passed away, so while I will never know the joy of being handled in his kitchen by his deft hands, it is still my aspiration to become incorporated into a gnocchi that would make Michael smile, perhaps, if my fortune allows, by one of his Friends Amid Food.

In Loving Memory
of
Michael Lane

Roasted Acorn Squash with Maple Syrup

Ingredients:

2 medium-sized acorn squash - cut top portion off and remove seeds

Olive oil to prepare pan

2 tablespoons unsalted butter

2 tablespoons dark brown sugar

4 tablespoons good maple syrup

1 teaspoon freshly grated nutmeg

1/2 teaspoon salt

1/4 cup chopped walnuts

Preparation: Preheat oven to 450 degrees

1) Line cookie sheet with foil. Using your hands, rub olive oil over foil to prevent squash from sticking during roasting.

2) Set four squash halves on baking sheet and top each with 1/2 tablespoon of the butter, 1/2 tablespoon of the brown sugar, 1/4 teaspoon of the nutmeg and 1/8 teaspoon of the salt.

3) Bake in preheated oven for 45 minutes until fork tender but not so soft shells collapse.

4) When done, remove pulp and spoon into a large mixing bowl. Taste for additional seasoning, if needed. Once seasoning has been adjusted, spoon mixture back into the individual squash.

5) Drizzle 1 tablespoon of the maple syrup over each and return to oven baking for another 10 - 15 minutes until squash are golden brown.

6) Garnish each squash with chopped walnuts before serving.

Makes four 4-ounce servings

Autumn Bouillabaisse

Ingredients:

2 tablespoons olive oil

1 leek - well cleaned and sliced

1 small to medium pumpkin - fresh only

1 Spanish onion - chopped

1/2 teaspoon dried fennel seeds

2 cups low-sodium vegetable or chicken broth

1/2 lb. shrimp - shelled and deveined

2 tablespoons fresh parsley - chopped

1/2 cup clam juice

2 cups canned whole tomatoes

1/2 cup white wine - slightly dry preferred

1 pinch saffron

2 teaspoons fresh thyme - leaves pulled from stemsSalt and pepper to taste

1/2 lb. fresh clams-cleaned and bearded or 1 cup canned clams

2 cups assorted meaty white fish (Halibut, Pacific Snapper, Rock Fish, Mahi Mahi) cubed

Preparation   Preheat oven to 375 degree

1) Clean and cut the pumpkin into large sections. Rub well olive oil and season with kosher salt and pepper. Place on a large, foil lined cookie sheet. Roast cut pumpkin for about 20-30 minutes until fork tender, but not mushy soft.

2) While pumpkin is roasting, heat the measured olive oil in a large, heavy cast-iron pot.

3) Add sliced leek and chopped onion, sauté until translucent, about 5 minutes.

4) Stir in canned tomatoes, breaking them up, by squeezing each tomato in your hand before dropping it into the pot. Reserve juice from can to thin soup if needed.

5) Add clam juice, broth, wine, fennel and saffron.

6) Bring mixture to a gentle boil, then immediately reduce heat and allow soup to simmer for about 30 minutes.

7) When pumpkin is done roasting and cool enough to handle, remove rind and cut large sections down into bite-sized portions adding to soup along with the fresh clams and shrimp.

8) Simmer another 5-7 minutes, being careful not to overcook seafood.

9) Add fresh chopped parsley and thyme just prior to serving.

10) Season with salt and pepper to taste.

Makes twelve 4-ounce servings

Autumn Apple Crisp

Ingredients for the apple mixture:

9 apples - 3 each; Baldwin or Braeburn, Granny Smith or Gravenstein, Rome Beauty or Gala. All apples should be rather large and firm with no bruising.

1/4 cup freshly squeezed lemon juice

1/4 cup all-purpose flour

1 tablespoon fresh lemon zest

1/2 cup golden raisins

3/4 cup granulated sugar

For the topping:

1½ sticks cold unsalted butter - cut into small cubes

1 teaspoon allspice

1¼ cup light brown sugar

1/2 cup all-purpose flour

2 tablespoons fresh lemon zest

1 teaspoon kosher salt

1 tablespoon cinnamon

1 tablespoon nutmeg

1½ cups steel cut oats - ground in food processor (but not to a powder)

Preparation: Preheat Oven to 375 degrees

1) Prepare 9 x 13-inch casserole dish with softened butter or cooking spray

2) Peel and slice all apples into wedges or rounds whichever you prefer.

3) Place prepared apples into very large glass or other non-reactive mixing bowl and squeeze fresh lemon juice over apples immediately to prevent browning.

4) Gently stir in all-purpose flour, lemon zest, sugar and raisins. Set bowl aside until ready to use.

To prepare topping:

1) In medium mixing bowl cut cold butter into flour

2) Add brown sugar, ground oats, salt, lemon zest, cinnamon, nutmeg and allspice

3) Pour apple mixture into casserole dish - spread oat topping all over top of apple mixture.

4) Bake until brown and bubbly - about 30 to 40 minutes. You may top each serving with dollop of ice cream and drizzle a bit of Irish whiskey over the top.

Makes twelve 4-ounce servings

Gnocchi with Sage Butter Sauce

Ingredients:

3 cups freshly prepared, and still hot mashed potatoes - recommend using Yukon Gold, with skins removed then put through a food mill. A potato ricer or regular potato masher will work too. Do not use a hand-mixer this may over-process the potatoes and release too much gluten, making for a tough dough.

1½ cups all-purpose flour + additional for working the dough

3 large eggs - 2 of them separated

1½ teaspoon kosher salt

1/4 teaspoon white pepper

Pinch of nutmeg

1 tablespoon olive oil

2-3 tablespoons melted unsalted butter

1½ cups freshly grated Parmesan cheese/save remaining wedge of cheese for garnish

For the Sage Butter Sauce

4 healthy leaves of fresh sage

3 tablespoons unsalted butter

Preparation:

1) In large mixing bowl, combine the hot mashed potatoes, flour, salt, pepper, nutmeg and olive oil, blending with a fork or pastry fork.

2) Add 2 eggs, 1 yolk only and the other whole egg with the white and mix thoroughly. If the dough feels too dry add the other egg yolk.

3) Turn the dough out onto a well-floured board or clean counter and knead gently about 14 times.

4) The dough should feel firm but yielding. If too soft add just a pinch more flour

5) Shape the dough into one fat and happy loaf setting on floured area to prevent sticking.

6) Separate the loaf into four equal sections, covering sections with a slightly damp paper towel.

7) Working with one section at a time, roll on lightly floured surface into 3/8-inch thick cord. Cut the cord of dough into 1 ½-inch lengths

8) Using a gnocchi board or dinner fork held at a 45-degree angle roll each gnocchi away from you to create the indentation pattern. As you finish each piece set off to the side in a single-layer and

dust with very lightly with flour. Continue this pattern until all the dough has been cut, rolled and formed in gnocchi puffs.

9) To cook; use a large heavy saucepot filled with gently boiling salted water and drop in about 14 to 21 gnocchi at a time. When gnocchi float to the surface (it takes about 1 minute) they are ready to be removed, using a slotted spoon or spider, and placed in a bowl that allows excess water to drain. Keep bowl covered to stay warm as you prepare the rest of the dough.

Sage Butter Sauce:

1) Heat the unsalted butter in a small, heavy saucepot until it turns the color of light hazelnut (this is known as beurre noisette).

2) Remove from heat and add minced sage leaves. It is best to mince the leaves just before adding them to the butter to avoid bruising. Allow the sage to infuse the butter as you arrange the prepared gnocchi in individual bowls or on a large serving platter.

3) Pour prepared sage sauce over warm gnocchi and shave additional Parmesan cheese over the top. Garnish with additional whole sage leaves if desired.

Makes eight 4-ounce servings

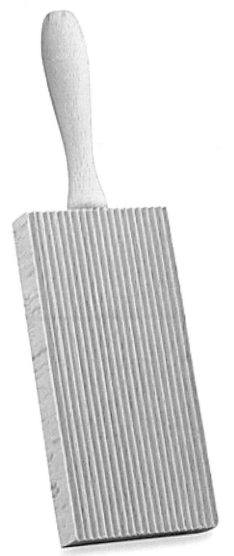

Where's The Beef? (what's more, who cares?) - December

The French animated character Remy from the movie *Ratatouille* had not been invited. But if he had known about this event, he would have surely designed a way to wiggle and shimmy his invertebrate self under the doorway. The December supper club event, hosted by Patrice and boyfriend/professional chef Bryant, was as satisfying as it was transformative. There was a round of thanks by more than a couple supper club members for this month's co-hosts going above, beyond and outside the cattle ranch when the invitations indicating a meatless theme were received.

This month's cuisine? Vegetarian French. Out of respect and in honor of Patrice's vegetarian diet, this supper club event was in adherence of her gastronomical preferences. The task initially appeared a bit daunting to those carnivores among the group. Even Rose, famous for her creative accommodations in the kitchen, had to admit the thought of French cuisine minus the duck confit or any larding, seemed undoable. But the undertaking was none too overwhelming for those Friends familiar with eye-opening films such as *Food Inc.*, *Forks Over Knives*, and other fiendish food exposés, enhancing the public's awareness of questionable practices in farming and food manufacturing. It was Patrice and Bryant's intention to prove meals accommodating vegan diets and clean eating can be flavorful and soulful. This month's supper club would provide Patrice and Carla validation and support along with a little incentive for the other members.

As it turned out, this particular gathering was an inadvertent misfortune for those who were absent. It was obvious from the moment the Friends walked over the threshold and onto the landing at the top of the stairs this was going to be a meal of never-before-seen meatless heights. As soon as they entered the small apartment, the first arrivals began inhaling the scent of sweet caramelized onions and a congenial broth.

When suddenly hit by this aromatic drift, Gilda's taste buds began to expand so wide her salivary glands watered to the point of creating a wash of saliva that made her speech sound gushed when she opened her mouth to say hello. She turned an heirloom tomato red while apologizing, frantically trying to swallow in order to avoid the sensation of drowning. Rose looked at her sister and was horrified as Gilda looked, for a brief moment, like a five-and-dime squirt gun while sounding like a gurgling brook.

"Swallow," Rose whispered curtly.

"I'm trying," Gilda winced and smiled weakly as Colin walked over to greet her with a hug.

The wine was served first, as would be customary for a French-themed meal. Patrice had already opened and allowed for breathing, a mature Pinot Noir, which exhibited a complexity of characteristics that included chocolate, figs and truffles. The wine was a perfect pairing for James's vegan Mediterranean terrine, a complicated appetizer even by his standards, involving the layering of grilled eggplant and sweet red bell peppers, along with homemade cashew cheese and fresh parsley.

"Well worth the effort James," complimented Bryant.

As Patrice continued filling wine glasses, there was much discussion regarding the difficulties in cultivating the Pinot vine since it is considered adaptable but also rather unstable. Colin explained that this often results in a good-sized gap between a high quality and low quality Pinot Noir, but everyone agreed Patrice and Bryant had made a very good selection. It was upon this mutual consensus that the Friends Amid Food sat down to the most classical of classic beginnings, French onion soup.

Chef Bryant's rendition was dark and earthy minus any heavy aftertaste. He served the individual crocks, each one looking like a small volcano, with a bubbling of broth doing its best to emerge from a coating of perfectly crispy, crusty cheese and capped with a golden brown crouton.

"Gilda, I don't think you'll have any trouble enjoying this soup," beamed Rose as Bryant placed her serving down in front of her. Gilda leaned over to better inhale the aromatic steam making its way to freedom from the bowl.

"I thought this was a vegetarian meal, Bryant," she murmured eyeing the soup suspiciously.

"It is," he replied.

"Then why does this smell like you used beef stock or broth?"

Bryant explained, as he sat down to join his guests, that in order obtain this tone and flavor, he made a severe reduction of vegetable broth, bourbon and vegetarian Worcestershire sauce.

"Vegetarian Worcestershire sauce?" asked Maureen. "I never heard of it."

"Neither have I," stated Jonah.

"I have, and I assume you have as well, Rose," chimed in James.

"Yes, I have. It's more of a vegan Worcestershire sauce. Right Patrice?" answered Rose.

"Yup. No anchovies in this. Actually it's really easy to prepare from scratch if you wanted to," Patrice continued. "It's just a mixture of apple cider vinegar, tamari or soy sauce, brown sugar and a couple of other seasonings. Very easy."

Bryant went on to share he opted out of using sherry, telling his eager listeners by substituting the sherry for bourbon allows the round full-bodied flavor of the clear-eyed consommé to express itself, all the while avoiding the sweeping overtones of sweetness that are so common in your average French onion soup.

Gilda's serving was minus the oversized crouton, so she was free to enjoy the conglomeration of broth, onions and cheese.

The soup course was followed by Maureen's incredible Ratatouille. She stayed true to French tradition, combining fresh eggplant, tomatoes, onions, zucchini, garlic and herbs. Green bell peppers were a personal omission. As it turned out, no one at the table claimed to have any  kind of commitment to them anyway. The bounty of vegetables, an obvious exploitation of Maureen's patio garden, were the stars of this dish. Maureen was careful to avoid any kind of distracted over-seasoning or useless additions. The inclusion of a warm baguette allowed all the guests to soak up the wonders of her amiable stew.

Jonah's contribution to the meal was an aesthetic , yet obviously palpable, potatoes au gratin.

"And NO butter," Jonah announced.

"No butter?! Why you seem proud, Jonah." Rose was astonished. "Really, no butter at all? You would never know."

Jonah's au gratin was copiously rich in taste and texture, still Rose could not help but ask, "What would Julia say, with no butter?"

"Most likely 'mmmm'," Carla replied.

All the other heads at the table nodded in agreement. Jonah's potatoes offered that very best of food combinations, simplicity with overall excellent flavor.

"No offense Jonah, but I'm going to skip the potatoes. There's so much good stuff here I need to choose wisely," confessed Gilda.

"Don't worry Gilda, Jonah's not offended. We completely understand and I concur. We have set before us a table of perennial pleasures," Colin replied.

As the table mates were savoring the closing of their love affair with this basic starch in one of its highest forms, Bryant rose from the table and returned carrying a platter of beautifully steamed asparagus spears. They were dressed along the skirt-line with fresh, small diced tomatoes, red onions and crumbles of goat cheese, the visual presentation resembled a unique kind of chorus line.

Gilda reminded the Friends that asparagus are, in reality, finger food. She was the first to joyfully extend her arm across the table to pick up and bite into one of the bright green javelins. The crisp crunch of the perfectly steamed al dente lance, made a pleasant snap between her teeth, then was cushioned by the sprinkling of soft chevré and diced tomatoes Bryant had adorned the asparagus with. The others watched and waited, as she slowly chewed and swallowed, then graciously licked her "utensils," the tips of her fingers. Gilda declared the asparagus were a triple play of taste, crisp, snappish vegetable, sweet, acidic tomatoes and decisive red onions followed by the salty-smoothness of chevré cheese. At that, the others immediately reached for the remaining green gams, dismantling chef Bryant's composed display.

Carla jumped from her seat. "Oh! I almost forgot! My mushrooms." Carla had almost forgotten about her stuffed mushrooms, still warming in the oven awaiting their own introduction. She quickly ran to the kitchen, which was only seven steps away and returned presenting each guest with his or her own individual plate upon which sat three small, piping hot mushrooms. The trio of fungi were huddled together emitting an aroma of forest and herb. As she set down each serving, Carla explained she often prepared one large Portobello mushroom stuffed to the brim with a salad on the side creating a complete and healthy meal for herself. Gilda made note of that for her own future use.

"But for supper club, I decided to serve baby Portobellos for a more repetitive and concentrated bang of taste. Besides, I like the way they look on these small plates, Carla explained."

She succeeded in banging off good taste with this ancient and often elusive food item. Without even allowing the mushrooms a moment to cool, she showed her food companions how to "pop the Portobello." The temperature of those fleshy and earthy buttons with their new-found French Provencal attire were still so hot her fellow diners had to literally tousle the little bites around inside their mouths to prevent burning their tongues. Yet it was with their tongues that they were able to taste the curative powers of butter, garlic, olive oil and the umami nuance of these festooned mushrooms.

To maintain the evening's theme, Rose stuck to her well-practiced quiche - a gift she was given, or more accurately, had wrestled out of Chef Laurence while working under his tutelage at his bakery. Even Chef Laurence, if he were to be offered a slice of this adaptation of his original, would not have balked at the exclusion of a flaky crust or the smoky, salty bacon he had taught Rose to efficiently whisk into the egg and cream mixture. This was, after all, a meatless meal, and as usual Rose was accommodating her sister's inability to consume bread-like foods. In place of bacon, Rose opted to use sweet roasted red bell peppers with paper-thin slices of fresh zucchini that had been just barely introduced to a sauté pan of butter and minced garlic. She used Fines herbs for seasoning. Her quiche was light and fluffy then baked to a subtle golden brown. It was an exceptional presentation of this classic northeastern French pie.

Where Gilda was free to indulge, Patrice was not, as the consumption of egg is not within the boundaries of her vegan diet.

"Well, you ate my serving of the ratatouille, so I'll eat your slice of quiche." Gilda said, smiling at Patrice.

By this time, the Friends Amid Food were on their third bottle of wine, a creamy, buttery Chardonnay, Stag's Leap, Bryant's declared favorite. This selection was consistent with the last two courses of the meal. The Friends had taken a brief intermission from eating as they finished emptying their wine glasses and chatted abiding by the French tradition of dining rather than rushing through the meal. Eventually they felt ready for dessert.

The offering was soft, yet held substantial body. It was opulent but did not overwhelm the palate. The balanced coupling of rich heavy cream and the seductive orchid, from which vanilla is derived, was a union appreciated by even the most serious of French food critics sitting at the table that evening. That would be Maureen and Carla.

When Gilda realized what was in store for them she became so excited she couldn't help herself. She burst into song singing *Tradition*! However, it was pointed out to her by Jonah that song was from the musical *Fiddler On The Roof* which is not French but Greek.

"Oy vey," laughed Colin. "But hey! Greek food and Tevye would be a great supper club food theme."

The Friends Amid Food sat comfortably at the table yet could easily see into the small apartment kitchen. They watched the capable hands of their hosts work together as Bryant and Patrice torched the sugar that was sprinkled atop the crème brûlée. There was no question this *pièce de résistance* was going to be sublime.

Patrice and Bryant placed a small ramekin in front of each friend. One by one, the Friends were overcome with childlike glee in cracking the hardened-caramelized sugar with the tips of their spoons. After breaking into and unlocking the protective cover that harbored the calorific custard that lay beneath, they slowly and deliberately slid their spoons in. The first mouthful, and each one that followed, was an experience of sensorial pleasure between contrasting soft custard and hard candy. These two combinations played an insightful game of tag and touch within the interior of the mouth. Carla watched, mesmerized, as each Friend carefully licked off whatever bit had adhered to his or her spoon before dipping it back into the ramekin for more. It appeared as though they were actually eating in slow motion in order to extend the experience as long as they could.

"Okay, I'm sugar-free. But sitting here watching all of you is torturous. I need to take only a very small taste," Carla exclaimed. "I can't take just watching anymore."

"Well, I can't eat all of this," Gilda responded. "Here's a spoon. You can have a bite of mine. There is plenty left to share."

The Friends gathered in the living room to finish the meal with snifters of warmed Grand Marnier, commenting on the bounty and grandeur of the food that came from the small and intimate kitchen. They all shared a brief moment of sorrow for those supper club members who were not able to join them for Vegetarian French that evening.   But there was only a smidge of sadness when they recalled the additional share of portions some chose to enjoy.   And as usual, there was plenty to take home. This was, indeed, a unique and special meal - there was nothing lacking or missed in the evening's menu. There was only creativity and the celebration amongst those Friends Amid Food, gathered at the table.

French Onion Soup

Ingredients:

4-5 onions, thinly sliced

3 tablespoons unsalted butter + 2 tablespoons

3 tablespoons all-purpose flour

2 quarts vegetable broth

1/2 teaspoon vegetarian Worcestershire sauce

1½ teaspoons fresh cracked pepper

12 slices buttered and toasted baguette slices

1/2 cup each, grated Parmesan and Gruyere cheese

1 tablespoons olive oil

2 sprigs fresh thyme

1/2 cup brandy

1/2 cup bourbon

Preparation: Preheat oven to 350 degrees

1) Heat olive oil and butter in a large heavy saucepot or Dutch oven. Add sliced onions and sauté until they caramelize to a rich, dark brown, but not scorched.

2) Add brandy, bourbon and Worcestershire sauce and thyme sprigs, cooking over medium heat until liquid is reduced by half.

3) Using a slotted spoon, remove the thyme sprigs and sprinkle the onions with the flour. Continue stirring until the starchiness is cooked out of the flour. About 10 minutes.

4) Pour in vegetable broth, season to taste with salt and pepper. Continue cooking over low heat for another 30 minutes.

5) While soup is simmering, brush baguette slices with remaining 2 tablespoons butter, melted, on both sides and arrange in a single layer on a baking pan. Place in a 350-degree oven until toasted to a golden brown. Set aside until ready to use.

6) When soup is ready to serve, ladle into individual serving crocks and top each with a toasted crouton. Add a handful of the grated cheeses on top of each crock or ramekin and set on a rimmed baking sheet.

7) Heat in oven broiler just until cheese is melted. Serve immediately.

Makes twelve 4-ounce servings

Dancing Legs Asparagus

Ingredients:

1 bunch thick asparagus spears-woody bottoms snapped off and trimmed with potato peeler

1/2 large red onion - sliced into rounds

3 tablespoons olive oil

1 tablespoon fresh lemon juice

2 cloves garlic - minced

1 teaspoon kosher salt

1/2 teaspoon fresh cracked pepper

4 ounces goat cheese - crumbled

1 large or 2-3 medium fresh tomatoes, diced

Preparation: Preheat oven to 425 degrees

1) Line jelly roll pan with aluminum foil and place cleaned asparagus and sliced onion in center of pan.

2) Drizzle olive oil over asparagus and onion then sprinkle with salt, pepper and minced garlic - toss to coat.

3) Spread asparagus and onion out evenly on pan and place in oven.

4) Roast for 12-15 minutes, until edges are just barely browned.

5) Remove from baking sheet and arrange on large platter in "leggy" fashion.

6) Scatter sliced tomatoes along bottom of asparagus.

7) Sprinkle crumbled goat cheese generously all over asparagus.

8) Squeeze fresh lemon juice over entire platter and serve.

Makes approximately six 4-ounce servings

Stuffed Mushrooms

Ingredients:

16-20 baby Portobello mushrooms, brushed clean of dirt, stems removed - don't discard stems - finely chop stems for use in stuffing

2 tablespoons unsalted butter + 2 additional tablespoons - melted

1 tablespoon olive oil

1/4 cup chopped fresh parsley

1 large shallot - minced

4 cloves fresh garlic, minced

2/3 cup white wine

1/2 cup vegetable broth-more if needed

5 ounces garlic & herbs cheese, (Boursin)

1-2 tablespoons bread crumbs

Preparation:

1) Heat butter and olive oil in skillet over medium heat. Add shallots and minced garlic until translucent and fragrant

2) Carefully pour in wine and broth. Bring to gentle boil - reduce heat and simmer uncovered about 15 minutes.

3) While liquid is simmering, clean and remove stems from mushrooms. Chop stems and place in medium mixing bowl. Add garlic-herb cheese to chopped stems, half the chopped parsley and just enough bread crumbs to create sufficient filling for mushrooms.

4) Transfer liquid to 3-4 quart au gratin dish, rectangular baking dish or oval casserole dish, lightly greased with butter

5) Spoon mushrooms with filling and place in casserole dish.

6) Bake uncovered in 425-degree oven 10 - 12 minutes.

7) When ready to serve drizzle with the 2 tablespoons melted butter and sprinkle with remaining chopped parsley.

Makes six to eight 4-ounce servings

Crustless Quiche with Salmon and Fresh Dill

This is a great way to use up leftover salmon. Or you may prepare a freshly cooked salmon specifically for this dish if you prefer.

Ingredients:

1 cup cooked salmon (roasted, baked or left-over)

4 eggs   1 to 1½ cups half and half

1/4 cup sour cream   1/4 cup softened cream cheese

1 teaspoon chopped fresh dill   1/8 teaspoon grated nutmeg

1/4 cup grated Swiss or Gruyere cheese   1/8 teaspoon white pepper

1 tablespoon Dijon mustard   1/4 teaspoon kosher salt

1 commercially prepared or homemade pie crust   1 teaspoon fresh lemon zest

Preparation: Preheat oven to 350 degrees

Note: Preparing a crust is optional. Rose, Gilda and the Friends Amid Food did not include a crust at their dinner party.

1) Prepare a 9" round, deep-pie or quiche pan by buttering or spraying with non-stick spray. Carefully unroll pie crust into pie pan.

2) In large mixing bowl, whisk together eggs, half and half, cream cheese, sour cream, grated cheese, salt, pepper, dill and nutmeg.

3) Brush bottom of pie crust with Dijon mustard.

4) Pour egg-cheese mixture into pan.

5) Top with salmon and lemon zest.

6) Bake 35-40 minutes until set - transfer to cooling rack.

Makes eight 4-ounce servings

The Blue Door - January

Carla:

Our heavy, planked door is made of Sugar Pine (I love those two words together; sugar pine) and is eye catching. Last year, I painted it a striking robin's egg blue. The door is adorned with an ornate, black wrought iron handle and matching hinges. Though I rather liked the weathered appearance of the door as it was, I had decided to paint it anyway, envisioning the entry of our home as a reflection of the colors we see in the sky above and the lake view outside. It would serve as a kind of focal point where these two great entities, the expanse of surrounding atmosphere and the ever-moving water of the lake, come together right here in front of our cottage.

Currently I am standing on the threshold of the doorway looking out at the lake, with our blue door wide open behind me. Inside, my husband is contentedly reading his newspaper. He's a throwback, one of those who still enjoy holding books and newspapers in his hands, inhaling the scent of the ink as he alternately moves the oversized pages from right hand to left. There has long been standing a stack of medical journals along with other precariously balanced mounds of reading on the floor surrounding his oversized, worn, latte-colored, leather chair. He promises me he'll get to them eventually. I'm not holding my breath.

This small house, like all our others before it, is lined with windows allowing the light and warmth from the sun to come streaming through, or when the weather changes, shrouds us in a soft blanket of gray clouds settling comfortably in our living room. Today the windows allow an abundance of warm sunlight to pass through. So it seems odd to me my husband has turned on his floor lamp. I say nothing, as we have been married many years and some things just don't need to be said aloud. Instead I announce that I am going to take a walk along the lake before preparing for tonight's supper club gathering. My husband peers up over his paper, smiling at me and nods his head, murmuring, "That's fine Carla, take your time."

I'm struck after twenty years of marriage he still takes the time to actually put down his reading, at least partially, and really look at me when I speak to him. I smile back in appreciation of his response and attentiveness. He believes I am smiling because I'm happy. He's right, I am happy today. There is little pain.

"I won't be long," I say and turn to go, leaving our blue door ajar inviting the sky and the lake to peek inside. I see this as a reimbursement of sorts for all the gazing out Gerard and I have enjoyed from our windows.

I gingerly walk down the gentle slope from our colorful cottage, unable to keep my head from turning to look back. It was not just the door to which I gave color. On the exterior I added wide bands of pastels in geometric patterns set in groupings of three. This mimics the art deco style beach homes I fell in love with during our trip to Miami Beach a few years ago.

Extending my gait, I carefully place only one foot on each of the worn, wooden steps winding their way towards the water. I am careful not to step on the succulent Elephant's Food (Portulacaria afra) that grows in the rocky sand between the slats and in some places is brave enough to sneak up and creep right onto the steps. It's obvious others before me have not been so careful, as some segments of plants have been broken and snapped.

In no time at all I reach the last step of the boardwalk and touch my booted feet down onto the strip of rocky sand and pebbles bordering the edge of the lake. The early sun is warm for January, but it is still early and the morning breeze feels chilly. I am always cold. I pull my heavy cable knit sweater around myself more tightly as I begin my walk.

I can't help but lift my face towards the sky and inhale the slightly fishy scent of the lake, listening to the movement of the water as it tenderly breaks on the shore. The sound reminds me of our dog Reinhart when he would lap up the water in his bowl. Reinhart passed away last year just before I decided the door needed painting. Gerard and I agreed we would get another dog after we had completed mourning our loss. We still don't have a new dog.

I am looking forward to tonight's dinner party. As hostess, I selected the theme Italian Fare Al Fresco knowing the weather will warm as the day progresses. I hope the wind will calm. I have been craving the energy and pleasure that comes with our gatherings. Since I have decided to host from my vacation home, our group will be smaller than usual due to the drive time required. But most of my Friends Amid Food are committed to going wherever there is the promise of good food and enthusiastic sharing.

I usually start my walks around the right side of the lake. Today I started to the left, hoping that the change of direction will cause a shift in my thinking. I am willing to do anything to break this block that has occurred in my writing. I am stuck in the third chapter which now only looks like a quagmire of words. I'm feeling desperate. I have a deadline. I am forever changing and revising words, phrases and entire chapters I was once relatively pleased with.

If I'm honest, I offered to host this month's supper club as more of a procrastination ploy. Can't write if I'm busy cooking and hosting. Who knows, someone may say or do something to inspire me. Something, anything. My exasperation has led me to resort to all kinds of ridiculous behaviors. The frustration I feel as a writer has caused me to over-think everything and fall into foul moods more often than usual. (An artistic Pisces, I have been accused of being moody.) A couple of weeks ago, my husband made a remark about my getting up on the wrong side of the bed. His sentence began and ended with "Carla" uttered as though my name was a superlative used when one has just whacked their thumb with a hammer.

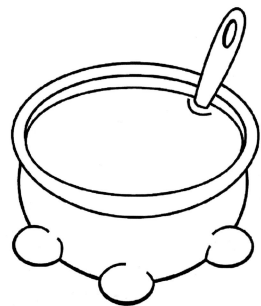

It was in that vein I thought perhaps there might be some merit in Gerard's statement. I apologized and promised to do my best to snap out of it. To show how sorry I was, that evening I prepared Gerard's favorite meatloaf with smashed potatoes and parsnips, homemade gravy and roasted Brussels sprouts. For dessert, lemon sorbet. I, of course, opted out of eating the meatloaf or potatoes. Instead I added another sheet pan to the oven and roasted plenty of fresh vegetables, along with a nicely seared cauliflower steak for myself. I did, however, take a couple bites of the sorbet. We both went to bed happy that night.

Gerard sleeps on the left side of our bed; I sleep on the right. The following morning, I awoke refreshed but that stuck feeling immediately washed over me like a rolling wave. I must have been dreaming of my writer's block. Yet, when I awoke, there was not a single new thought or idea for this writing project in my head, as is often the case after a good night's sleep. Nope, no dramatic dreams or visions, made their way from my subconscious to my conscience self.

On that particular morning, I woke very early, and decided to extend my daily walk beyond my usual one hour, with the intention of not even thinking about writing. I allowed my thoughts to drift, much like the small tree branch I spied moving along the river's flow, to a new fruit tart recipe I was in the process of creating. Plums and what? Plums and raspberries has been done to death. Plums and pears? I'd been trying out different combinations that would suit both Gerard and me. But I felt my face beginning to scowl as I struggled to keep my thoughts on recipes rather than writing. I was overcome with that grumpy feeling again within minutes, in spite of those visions of (sugar) plums or not, dancing in my head.

Then it occurred to me. Maybe I am getting up on the wrong side of the bed! I quickly turned around and rushed back to the cottage. Gerard was not yet up, I carefully crawled back into bed so as not to disturb him and laid down for a moment, just to make it count. Then, slowly, I lifted myself to a sitting position and began to wordlessly reach and climb over my husband so I could get out on the left (his) side of the bed. I have been doing this now for well over a week. Gerard, forever the trooper, pops his head up a bit and grabs a kiss as we are momentarily face-to-face during my exchanging of sides. He watches wordlessly as I engage in this new fandangled kind of yoga which begins with my rolling across our huge bed over to his side, as I prepare to dismount. I then straddle Gerard's torso, stretching and extending my body as far as my fifty-plus muscles and joints allow so I can exit, stage left. This ritual does not seem to be doing much for my creative process, but Gerard is certainly enjoying it.

In order to help dislodge this writer's block I've even resorted to pulling out old articles of clothing I wore when I was experiencing greater success in storytelling and writing. Hence, this tattered cable knit sweater. But this fashion effort doesn't seem to be working either. Instead, I'm just looking a bit ragged and dated. When my stepdaughters came up to the cabin for a short visit last week, the eldest concurred when her younger sibling blurted, "Well, Carla, you're old enough now that you can get away with it." I knew the comment was well intentioned and they laughed in a good spirited manner. I couldn't help but giggle about it myself. They're right, I am old enough to get away with it. "At least you're not wearing socks with flip-flops." I lowered my head. "Oh no! You are?" they screamed. However, I also know, the girls are somewhat glad about my aging. It seemed to bother them that I was several years younger than their mother.

This January morning as I continue around the water's edge, I quicken my gait as my thoughts segue to this evening's dinner. For my dish, I'm going to prepare a simple, yet full-flavored, grain-based salad, using one of my favored ingredients, eggplant. I've always considered eggplant a dark beauty among vegetables. Most people don't know eggplant is a member of the nightshade family and is related to the odious potato. For centuries, Europeans had thought potatoes to be poisonous and refused to eat them. Thank goodness that was debunked. For me, whether I am selecting those richly, purpled oblong tubers or the small Italian baby eggplant or even the egg-shaped white eggplant, I savor the taste, texture and versatility offered by this meaty victual.

Walking towards our local farmer's market, I anticipate there will be a bit of eyeball rolling behind my back regarding my outfit. I haven't mentioned I am also wearing an old pair of golfing capris that were once khaki-green in color, but are now so grayed, they only look dirty. Nonetheless, I've set my mind to scope out and select the very best eggplant, sweet grape tomatoes and a combination of fresh herbs. Hopefully, the vendor who offers his usual grand array of grains will be there. Suddenly I realize the sun is now much warmer and higher in the sky. I must have been walking for longer than I had intended, completely forgetting I told Gerard I wouldn't be long.

Supper Club

The Friends arrived at Carla's second home, a first visit for most of them, earlier than usual for supper club due to the travel time home. Almost immediately they were struck by the beauty of the lake and surrounding area. Even with the car windows open, it was very quiet, the only sound was that of the car tires crunching along the rocky driveway mimicking the sound one makes while eating a breakfast bowl of Grapenuts. As they approached the end of the drive, Gilda remarked she had forgotten how charming the cottage was. Earlier during the drive, she shared she had spent ten days at Carla and Gerard's cabin three years ago while participating in a fasting and meditation retreat they hosted about a year prior to her surgery. She said she was good for a couple of months afterward, but then the sights and sounds of nature and her visualization exercises finally gave way to her cravings for soup, bread and wine, and chocolate, of course.

The exterior of the cottage displayed a palette of colors in patterns of three that set it apart from the others, most of which were as weathered as Carla's home, but were more drab and less

tended to. The Friends all chatted in agreement, as they excitedly knocked on the bright blue door, that Carla's home exemplified a fictitious cottage set along the shore of the Eastern Seaboard. Colin pointed out a wooden, carved pelican sitting atop an old tree stump near the bougainvillea-covered trellis.

Within moments they were greeted by Carla wearing her tranquil, infectious smile. She looked a bit tired and pale but was energetic in her distribution of hugs. Colin and Jonah lingered in their embraces with her. It was obvious they were bothered by Carla's condition and its return. Carla graciously gave instructions as to where they were to place their prepared dishes and began pouring a Chianti Classico. She then offered to take them on a quick tour of the cottage which was an easy offer to accept. They were all interested in seeing the interior since the exterior was such a unique update, or rather, Carla's personal expression of art deco.

As their shoeless feet went pitty-pat from blue room to yellow room to seafoam green room they ooh'd and aah'd at Carla's original, yet uncomplicated approach to design, furnishings and accents. Paintings and photos of doors and windows from all over the world hung on contrasting yet complementary-shaded walls. Each Friend paused a little too long, looking at one particular photo of a large opened window. No screens or curtains were on the acrylic depiction of this window to hide what provided a direct view into what appeared to be a large, warm and inviting kitchen. Without being able to explain why, each Friend felt drawn into the painting. Their eyes almost straining to see past the watercolor kitchen into the other rooms of this picturesque home. It evoked a sense that it belonged to what appeared to be a traditional Italian family.

Perhaps it was the planter boxes spilling over with geraniums and the hints of the neighboring clean laundry billowing in the breeze painted into the corner of the canvas that led the viewers of this painting, to draw this conclusion.

They all stood, huddled together in Carla's bright study gazing as though, if they waited long enough, they would become privy to some movement or indication of what the residents were doing in the other rooms. Hoping their patience would be rewarded when the residents of the home would finally sense people were waiting for them to enter the kitchen.

Carla broke the spell by ushering us into another room of her home where there hung an oversized lithograph of a solitary bright yellow door. There was nothing else in this picture, only the slightly ajar, banana-colored entrance attached to a small or perhaps magnificent abode. Was this a door that provided entry to a home in some ethnically rich country?

"Where was this photo taken?" asked Patrice.

"Africa maybe," stated Gilda.

"Why do you say that?" asked Rose.

"I don't know it just feels like that's where it is."

"I'm not sure where the location of this door and its home is," Carla said. "You get to decide."

"Well it's very intriguing and pleasing at the same time," remarked Patrice.

The photos and paintings that hung in her home only added to their curiosity about their friend, Carla, and her history. Where did she grow up? None of them knew. Had she traveled to these foreign lands they saw in her collection of paintings and photos? Did she have favorite restaurants in these exotic locations? Did she take any cooking classes while visiting? She certainly seemed well-traveled. Rose began in earnest to ask a few of these questions, beginning with an inquiry about the artist of one of the paintings as they continued their tour.

Gilda answered for Carla by stating, "I bet her husband did it. He's an artist, right?"

Carla responded that it was she who used to paint. Her husband was a law professor who only had a great appreciation of art. None of the Friends had ever met her husband, nor would they tonight. Carla continued to explain, as they made their way down the hall, that Gerard had gone out for dinner and a movie with a few of his professor friends. "He deserves a break. He's been taking such good care of me and has been a real sport about eating clean with me."

She paused outside her laundry room to draw their attention to a muted oil painting. This one depicting a set of windows reflecting a man and a woman sitting alongside a river enjoying an abundant picnic arranged on the blanket they sat on accompanied by a tranquil and regal golden retriever sitting at the feet of the man.

"Is that you and Gerard?" asked Gilda.

"Well, not exactly us, it was more like we inspired the painting. It was done by one of our neighbors up the road a bit." A couple of the Friends began looking around for evidence of a dog.

"Oh so you have a dog?" inquired Colin.

"No," Carla answered flatly.

When the tour was complete, the group returned to Carla's rustic, yet gourmet-fashioned kitchen which could only be described as stunning. They began to refill their wine glasses, then turned to look outside. In unison, they simultaneously exhaled. Carla's outdoor kitchen patio softly lit with strings of white lights had been arranged in such a deliberate and well-planned manner, from place settings to centerpiece, it was obvious the meal was going to be an exploitation of the aura of comfort and detail, which they were beginning to learn, was the essence of Carla herself.

To whet their appetites, they remained gathered in the kitchen a little longer, enveloping themselves in the aromas of the dishes sitting covered in saucepots, serving bowls and platters awaiting their unveiling. The Friends stood at the kitchen counter chatting it up, waiting for the sun to go down and position itself to allow just the right amount of light to only gently assert itself over the patio, as that was Carla's directive. Only after the sun had resigned itself from bright shine to tempered twilight, thus creating an ambiance that wouldn't blind her guests, did Carla give the cue that dinner was to begin. One by one they uncovered and revealed their carefully prepared dishes, then plated up and reassembled themselves out on the patio to dine al fresco.

Rose began the meal with her introduction of a spot-on pasta e fagioli. This Italian soup has the reputation of being hearty, a kind of "stick-to-your-ribs" one-pot meal, so hearty at times, as Rose pointed out, there have been occasions where she's had to wash down every other spoonful with a gulp of water. Gilda agreed, sharing she was once served a very small bowl of the soup that afterwards left her feeling she had consumed a kind of paste intended to stick to her ribs for days. However, this was not the case with Rose's particular version. Rose told her dinner companions she had recently discovered another super grain, organic in nature and very low in gluten. It's called kamut which she went on to explain, is actually the Egyptian word for wheat. Rose explained she used kamut in place of the traditional orecchiette.

"Kamut means wheat? That's ironic, considering it's gluten-free," observed Colin.

"No, it's not gluten-free, only lower in gluten than most other grains. It's kind of like spelt." Carla interjected. Carla shared her expertise in the area of healthy food choices by explaining, kamut is a very high protein wheat that has never been hybridized. The kernels are up to two or three times larger than other wheat and have a much higher nutritional value.

"Where did you find it, Rose?" asked Maureen.

"I found it last week at the farmer's market. There's a vendor who always has the most unusual grains and pastas. I love him. He's originally from Tuscany and has been active in the Slow Food Movement. Very knowledgeable," Rose said.

"There's a vendor up here who sounds just like your guy. Maybe it's the same vendor." Carla wondered aloud.

Use of kamut gave Rose's fagioli a subtle nutty flavor without that paste and mortar effect Gilda had referred to. Her dish held the expression of true Italian flavors with her use of cannellini and green beans, onions, carrots, celery and Roma tomatoes, combined in a well-orchestrated broth with just the right amount of saltiness imparted by her immaculately small-diced cuts of prosciutto.

Next, Patrice, pregnant as ever but showing up with her game on, arrived lugging in her largest of Le Creuset Dutch-ovens. It was brimming with a rich and fragrant mushroom risotto. She admitted Bryant did assist, but Patrice's personal knowledge of what's required in the making of a voluminous risotto was obvious. She told of a full morning's worth of tending, stirring and slowly adding of the vegetable broth one ladle at a time, allowing the liquid to be fully absorbed, then slowly adding more liquid. Her efforts were well spent. Wild was her variety of mushrooms, tame was her seasoning. Bryant had instructed her to drizzle, ever-so-lightly, his prized white truffle oil just prior to serving. This only increased the urge to dive in  with their oversized pasta spoons and eat the risotto right out of the pot. Only Gilda showed restraint by spooning a small amount of the delightfully unctuous side-dish onto her plate.

Carla, on the other hand, redeemed herself from the disastrous misuse of a perfectly good eggplant last August. It happened with her preparation of thinly sliced, roasted eggplant spread with béchamel sauce and wrapped around large shrimp. The intention was to create a unique finger food for an outdoor concert a few of the Friends attend every summer. While the flavor combination was wonderful, heightened with the use of fresh rosemary, the mandolin sliced eggplant became soggy and slippery causing them to become insufficient to hold onto the shrimp that ended up sliding out at first bite along with the béchamel sauce that dripped its way out from the bottom. Unless they had securely affixed their teeth to the shrimp, those little crustaceans oozed their way out and one was left with a soggy slice of eggplant held in a béchamel coated hand.

Tonight, it was obvious Carla was not willing to barter her reputation as an accomplished cook. Her food contribution to the Italian al fresco evening was a main dish salad. During her dish introduction, Carla explained she had selected two good-sized eggplants, cut them medium-diced, then seasoned with good extra virgin olive oil, kosher salt and a blend of fresh Italian herbs cut from the artistic vertical planter covering an entire wall of her patio. Then lovingly, the Friends were sure, she grilled up these cubes of fruit (eggplant is actually a fruit with a dark history Carla told them) and tossed them with halved red and yellow grape tomatoes, toasted pignoli, garlic-herbed goat cheese and fresh basil. This Italian-themed salad could only be described as a mouthful of bold taste with a sensual combination of textures. The grilling of the eggplant added a layer of smokiness.

"Bravo Carla, grilling, always a good foundation to start with," declared Rose.

Maureen provided the proverbial Italian staple expected at every Italian meal: bread. She prepared from scratch a wonderful focaccia, lightly seasoned with coarse sea salt and dried herbs. Colin and Jonah laid claim to Carla and Gilda's share of bread after they saw Maureen had gone the extra mile for increased flavor with her addition of Greek olives baked into the bread. This traditional bread was simple and to the point, lighter than most and not a bit dry. Dryness was an attribute better suited to their wines that evening as Jonah continued to pour and talk. Without intention the conversation drifted into current affairs and politics. This is an area of discussion the artistic group of food friends didn't usually gravitate towards. It came about when Maureen sighed in a rather blissful manner and mentioned how lovely and warm it was in spite of the fact it was mid-January. This led to someone at the table exclaiming how the unseasonable warmth they were experiencing in January was due to global warming. Amid the bantering, Carla staunchly declared global warming was more about certain politicos instilling fear in the hearts and minds of the general public while collecting money in their pockets.

"Certainly no one can deny that things are warming up and icebergs are melting, but this is simply a natural cycle. Not global warming," she stated.

The conversation came to an abrupt halt and there was a momentary silence but no feelings were hurt and no offense was taken by the inadvertent exploration into the political differences between Friends who are deeply attached to one another by their passion for food.

After the discussion had calmed and returned to a level of hot-topic restraint induced by Rose, it was time for another food introduction. Colin and Jonah chose not to divert from central Italian custom by preparing a pasta dish. They started with homemade fettuccini.

"Homemade pasta is not nearly as difficult as people think," imparted Jonah.

"Well, it can be a bit messy, but Jonah's right. Whether or not you have a pasta machine or attachment for your stand mixer, it's just flour, oil, egg and water," explained Colin

"Not just all-purpose flour though, it's best to include some semolina flour," injected Jonah.

The boys took turns detailing the remaining ingredients of their dish; beefy canned San Marzano tomatoes which they had encouraged to merge with roasted butternut squash, Italian sausage and dark bone-in, chicken thighs. When the lid was removed from the largest of cast iron Dutch ovens, another substantial one-pot entrée was integrated with the other dishes. While whole-hearted in taste, this dish was not so heavy as to deter anyone except Gilda from enjoying its audacious addition to their dinner. This contribution from Jonah and Colin was the perfect accompaniment to their third bottle of wine.

An hour and a half later, the meal came to an end with the BEST cannoli any of them had ever tasted. Truly, this fabulous dessert prepared by their hostess, consisted of only "good chocolate," fresh orange zest and "high quality, high fat, ricotta," Carla offered no more information than that. It was clear they were not going to be given this recipe. Carla did share that her crispy, crunchy shells were prepared from scratch, which only added to the superior taste experience of a sweet brittle shell with a tangy cheese filling. It was nice that her shells were not so fragile as to cause the pastry to end up as broken shards scattered all over the laps of her guests. In Carla's opinion that would have been a waste of perfectly good cannoli. Carla's dessert was a delightful contradiction in that her rich, tart, creamy cheese filling was laced with semi-sweet miniature chocolate chips inside. What a difference love and attention to detail can make to food. Every dish created and shared among the Friends during this supper club confirmed that edict. They all thoroughly enjoyed themselves with lively, political conversation and an inspired meal.

Dinner lasted longer than it was meant to. As it was later than anyone realized when they finally made their way out to the cars. Looking back at Carla as she stood standing on the threshold of her blue door, the Friends realized tonight's supper club offered more than good food. They also got a more intimate glimpse of a before now, rather reticent supper club member, a member who has more to offer than just fabulous recipes (not all of which she is willing to share) with warmth and

kindness few of them knew she possessed. There was now even greater appreciation of the artistry and heart that each of them incorporates into the dishes offered at these monthly gatherings.

They shouted their thanks to this month's hostess and turned to walk down her long driveway to their cars, each taking a moment to view the nearly full moon casting its reflection on the lake.

As their caravan of two cars drove back down the gravel drive, they saw the headlights of an oncoming car. They could barely make out the outline of a bearded man wearing some type of cap or beret. Though it was difficult to see him clearly, they were just able to make out that he was smiling and rather handsome.

"Must be Gerard," said Gilda.

"I don't even know him and I can tell I like him." replied Rose.

"Yeah, I feel the same way. What a great couple," added Patrice.

"I hope she gets better soon," murmured Gilda, as she turned around to watch Carla wave goodbye from the dimly lit porch in front of the blue door.

Pasta e Fagioli with Kamut

Ingredients:

4 sprigs fresh thyme

4 sprigs fresh rosemary

1 fresh bay leaf

1 cup kamut berries - rinsed

1 tablespoon olive oil

1 tablespoon unsalted butter

3 ounces pancetta - chopped (optional)

1 medium Spanish onion - chopped

1 large carrot - small diced

1 large leek - cleaned and small diced

2 cloves fresh garlic - minced

Pinch red pepper flakes

4 cups vegetable broth

1 can kidney beans - drained

1 can cannellini beans - drained

1 14-ounce can San Marzano tomatoes

salt and pepper to taste

1/2 cup shaved Parmesan cheese

1/2 cup fresh chopped parsley (for garnish)

Additional olive oil if needed

Special Tools: Cheese cloth and kitchen twine

Preparation:

1) Prepare a bouquet garni by cutting a 6" x 6" square of the cheese cloth. Place thyme, rosemary and bay leaf in center of square, gather corners together and tie with closed with kitchen twine. Set aside until ready to use.

2) Rinse kamut by placing measured portion into a bowl; pour boiling water over the top. Allow to sit for about 30 minutes, then rinse. Set aside until ready to use.

3) Heat the tablespoon of olive oil and butter in a large, heavy Dutch oven.

4) Add pancetta, onion, carrot and leeks – sauté about 3 minutes until soft and translucent.

5) Add garlic and pepper flakes – sauté another minute.

6) Using a wooden spoon (as that is the traditional Italian tool), stir in broth, beans, and canned tomatoes. Use your hands to squeeze and break up each tomato before dropping it into the pot. Reserve the tomato juice in case you need to thin out the soup later.

7) Add the bouquet garni of herbs and season the soup with salt and pepper to taste.

8) Bring the mixture to a boil, then stir in kamut and reduce the heat to simmer and cook another 30 minutes.

9) Using a slotted spoon, remove bouquet garni bag and test for additional salt and pepper if

needed. Or if soup has thickened too much add a little of the tomato juice.

10) Ladle into individual serving bowls and garnish each with chopped parsley, shaved cheese and a drizzle of olive oil.

Makes eight 4-ounce servings

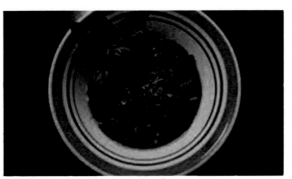

Mushroom Risotto

Ingredients:

2 tablespoons unsalted butter

3-4 cups vegetable broth - warmed on the stove

1½ cups Arborio, Vialone or Bomba rice

1/2 cup dried Porcini mushrooms

1/2 cup Crimini mushrooms - halved

1-2 tablespoons fresh chives - chopped

1/2 cup baby Portobello mushrooms - halved

1/2 cup fresh parmesan cheese - grated

1 tablespoon olive oil

1 clove garlic - minced

Salt and pepper to taste

1/4 cup pine nuts - toasted

zest of one lemon

1 medium shallot - minced

1/4 cup dry white wine

1 teaspoon truffle oil

Preparation:

1) Melt butter with the olive oil in a large, heavy saucepot.

2) Add minced garlic and shallot cooking just until fragrant - careful not to burn.

3) Stir in the rice and cook until well coated and just barely golden in color.

4) Slowly stir in wine.

5) Add mushrooms, large ones quartered, smaller ones halved - sauté about 1 minute.

6) Begin to add broth 1 ladle at a time, with a pinch of salt and pepper, stirring continuously with a wooden spoon, allowing each cup of liquid to be completely absorbed before adding the next.

7) (This is where the "love" comes into your risotto - it's all about the stirring and tending.)

8) Continue stirring in ladles of broth cooking over low heat until rice has softened and risotto becomes thick and creamy.

9) Just before you add the last cup of broth, stir in half the zest of the lemon along with half of the grated cheese

10) When all the liquid has been added and the rice is tender, remove from heat adding fresh thyme and toasted pine nuts.

11) Season to taste with additional salt and pepper.

12) Pour into 8 individual serving bowls. Garnish each with remaining freshly grated lemon zest, grated cheese and truffle oil drizzled distributed over each serving.

Makes eight 4-ounce servings

Eggplant And Tomato Panzanella

Ingredients:

1 large eggplant - cut into bite-sized cubes

3 cups day-old French bread - cut into bite-sized cubes

1/4 cup olive oil + additional 1/2 cup

1 tablespoon Italian seasoning

1 small red onion - thinly sliced

1½ cups each, red and yellow cherry tomatoes - halved

1/2 cup Burata - sliced

Salt and pepper to taste

3 cloves fresh garlic - minced

1/2 cup good balsamic vinegar

7-10 leaves fresh basil - chiffonade

Preparation: Preheat oven to 350 degrees

1) Arrange sliced eggplant onto large sheet pan and drizzle lightly with 1/4 cup olive oil on both sides. On another large sheet pan, arrange cubes of day-old, cubed bread evenly in a single layer and drizzle with 1/4 cup olive oil. Sprinkle bread cubes evenly with Italian seasoning, salt and pepper. Using your hands, mix bread cubes to ensure all sides are coated with olive oil and seasonings.

2) Place both sheet pans into preheated oven. Roast eggplant until edges are crisp and slightly browned. Toast bread cubes until golden brown - you will have to stir the bread once half way through baking.

3) Meanwhile, in a small mixing bowl, whisk together the remaining 1/4 cup olive oil, balsamic vinegar and 1 of the minced garlic cloves. Season to taste with salt and pepper. Set aside until ready to use.

4) When eggplant and croutons are done baking and have cooled, place in a large serving bowl.

5) Gently stir in halved tomatoes, red onion slices, remaining cloves of minced garlic and half the basil chiffonade.

6) Pour olive oil and vinegar mixture over top and stir gently to coat.

7) Garnish top with remaining basil and sliced burrata.

Makes eight 4-ounce servings

Cajun Creole - March

Music and beads and pork - oh, my!

Most people don't realize Las Vegas can get very cold during the winter season. Because the elevation from 2,030 to 4,000 feet above sea level, it is considered high desert. And as such, on some occasions we get snowfall.

This so surprises those who believe Vegas temperatures hold in the 90's year round, Gilda never tires of forwarding photos of Las Vegas winters with snowcapped palm trees and the ordinarily dry desert shrubs laden with snow. She takes tremendous glee in adding captions like, "Where's Gilda - guess?" or "What's wrong with this picture?" One of everyone's favorites is a photo Gilda staged with Rose wearing a swimsuit, sunglasses and a wide-brim hat, all bundled up in winter coat and scarf standing under a heavily, snow-covered tree. For added drama, Gilda insisted Rose arrange herself on a beach towel with a flotation device and picnic basket beside her.

It was March, and in an effort to ward off the tiresome cold and constant winds, another indigenous component of Southern Nevada winters, Jim came up with a supper club theme he was sure would be embraced by the other members, a cuisine that would offer some heat and spice along with a celebratory feel. As host, Jim was thrilled about the prospect of offering his food companions something to shake off the winter doldrums.

At any time, depending upon the season, visitors approaching Jim's front door are sure to feel a tickle under their noses and myriad of delights for their eyes. Initially it is the scents they pick up on. It may be jasmine, gardenia, lavender, or mint. Without even realizing, they'll close their eyes, and inhale deeply. When they reopen, their eyes then feast upon purple and white wisteria, yellow trumpets and magenta colored "fireworks" also known as fountain grass shrubs. In spring these botanical varieties seem to smile as they boast life amid brown grasses and rows of barren miniature lemon, lime and fig trees. Only the pomegranate trees express themselves with color and fruit.

There is a raised bed of winter-strong, happy herbs displaying itself on the protected, sunnier side of his house. It is early March and not all that is planted in Jim's garden can yet show itself above ground. But the evidence of what is to become is clear. Should your eyes continue to scan the yard, you will see a collection of common gardening tools, various mismatched gloves, a well-used charcoal barbeque as well as other odd-looking, less familiar tools scattered about. It is obvious a gardener lives here. What is not so obvious, is that this resident gardener pours concrete by day and indulges his gardening, painting and cooking on weekends and during the off season. Concrete pouring is not a year-round endeavor.

Jimmy is an infrequent participant in the Friends Amid Food supper club, but as Rose's long-time friend, he is always given a warm welcome when he's able to join. According to Gilda, many years ago, Jim and Rose lived in a commune with other free-spirited types, when twenty-somethings had passions unrelated to technology or money, when Bob Dylan and Joan Baez were a couple. A time when people regularly raised two fingers up in a V-sign symbolizing "peace" among one another rather than the one-finger salute now so commonly seen on the hands of angry drivers racing by.

Sometimes, if the mixture of food and wine is just right, Jim and Rose share excerpts and stories about life in the commune and about a summer's trip they took hitchhiking across the country with another friend in tow. That spirit of personal freedom, bucking the system and playfulness is now only somewhat palpable in Rose, but is certainly evident in her dear friend Jimmy.

It was a windy and chilly day, and the temperatures had remained low for several days. Las Vegans don't handle cold well, so for this reason Rose was in complete agreement with Jim when he suggested a meal that included some heat. "Some food to warm the soul," Jim touted.

There had been a one-month lapse in the gatherings due to the Friends' loss of culinary comrade Michael, but tonight's grand response to attend supper club indicates the Friends Amid Food were ready to regroup with recipes and appetites.

In spite of the biting cold in the evening air, Jimmy's front door was wide open when the first of his guests arrive.

"Wow! It's warm in here," exclaimed Gilda as she entered the house.

"I know, nice huh? This Viking oven cranks out enough heat to warm an airplane hangar. I hope you're hungry, Gilda," Jim smiled as he gave Gilda a peck on the cheek following the passionate hug he gave Rose.

Jim himself is a man of small stature, almost hobbit-looking. He looks as though he has never taken a razor to the beard symbolizing his hippie days. It appears longer every time Rose and Gilda see him. His clothes are always casual and comfortable-looking, holey jeans and worn flannel shirts. Even when clean, his hands wear the dry chalky look of a man who is consistently immersed in in some kind of earthly staple, be it cement, soil, flour or paint. These are the elements that make up the man. At the moment Jim's hands are working with liquids as he hurriedly prepares a Naw'lins favorite, the "Hurricane."

"Gilda, I know you don't drink, but you might want a sip of this," Jim calls over his shoulder. "The Hurricane is a mixture of light rum, dark rum, passion fruit juice, orange juice and a couple of other syrupy additions," Jimmy educated his early arrivals as he poured, telling them the history of the Hurricane. John came through the open door next.

"John!" called out Jim to greet him and without skipping a beat continued. "John, did you know it was in 1939 when this tasty concoction, the Hurricane, was created by New Orleans tavern owner Pat O'Brian? During World War II, scotch and whiskey were the more popular choices of drink.

Even though Prohibition was already over, in 1933 I think it was scotch and whiskey that were hard to come by. Because of this, liquor purveyors would force bar owners to purchase about fifty cases of the less popular rum before they would even consider filling a single order for just one case of whiskey." Jim handed John a tall glass of the freshly prepared libation.

Jim continued, "Anyhow, it was in this vein that the bar owner, Pat O'Brian, came up with a way to get rid of as much of the popular rum as quickly as possible. After a little experimenting, tasting and more experimenting, he came up with the Hurricane. Pretty tasty way of unloading a whole lot of rum I'd say."

"Fascinating," said Gilda as she took a sip from John's glass, "You're right. This is damn good. It's sweet, like me. Can you make a virgin one, no rum?"

"Absolutely my sweet."

"Oh brother," remarked Rose smiling, as she rolled her eyeballs.

Jim shared with those huddled around him that the Hurricane is so closely associated with New Orleans and Mardi Gras, he didn't feel there could be any better beverage to cool the tongues of his foodie Friends, knowing they would be embarking upon cuisine famous for its andouille sausage, hot jambalaya, red beans and rice, and of course, that "other-other" white meat, alligator. Jim's offering of this tall, sweet libation served in the traditional, curvy glass was met with a resounding "yes" by all of his early arrivals.

Other Friends continued to stream through the door, joining Jim, John, Rose, Gilda and Maureen. Each was immediately greeted by a drink, a warm hug and spirited conversation. By the time the last of the Friends arrived many were already feeling the warmth prompted by the cocktails, the food warming in Jim's industrial oven and the spicy scent of the many dishes as they were set upon Jim's oversized, wooden farm table.

As the second round of Hurricanes blew through the room, the level of conversation rose to a rumble. There was a moment when the conversations came to a halt at the barking of Jim's dog announcing the arrival of the last guests, then resumed with "hi's" and "hey-there's" as supper club members Sophie and Kyle entered the kitchen carrying two large platters showcasing shrimp po'boys. This caused all eyes to widened and set mouths to watering. Jim's dog laid patiently on his worn, comfy pillow bed, his big brown eyes watching every move of the humans milling about his home, knowing he wouldn't have to wait long for a morsel or two to fall to the floor.

Sophie and Kyle unwrapped the platter. "Dig in guys, we made these po'boys in miniature so we can eat them as an appetizer. But you want them while they're still hot," directed Kyle.

"Wow, this is a great way to kick off dinner," garbled John, his mouth full of large, succulent shrimp pressed between two slices of warm crusty bread.

Kyle's seasoned fried shrimp was a combination of sweet and spicy, nestled between the slices of warmed sourdough. He and Sophie had efficiently tucked in crisp leaves of iceberg lettuce, pickle relish and rounds of ripe red tomato. The dollops of their zesty aioli was a tasty accent to the sandwich as everyone wordlessly crunched their way through their amuse-bouche. Jeremiah and Jimmy entertained the idea of making a meal of the po'boys alone with Jeremiah's home-brewed beer which was now making its way around the room. But they decided against it as they licked their fingertips, not wanting to deny themselves the promise of those indulgences yet to come.

"Here, Rosie, I put a couple of shrimp in a bowl for you to taste, no bread just shrimp and a little aioli." Sophie walked over to Rose who had been watching the boys enjoy their sandwiches. "How about you Carla, can I fix a small bowl for you too?"

"Oh god yes! Fix her a little bowl, this is the bomb!" exclaimed Gilda.

As the last of po'boys was consumed, with nothing falling to the floor for Jim's poor dog Remington, conversations resumed. The loudest being that of Jeremiah and Jim's on the how-to's of making home-brewed beer. Adding to the festive bantering were Bryant and Rose who chatted on about the selection of wines Diana and Shelly were pouring to complement the anticipated "kick" of the evening's cuisine.

Finally, it was time to gather around Jim's notched and carved table to introduce the dishes. When John removed the sealed Dutch oven lid of his jambalaya, a geyser of aromatics burst forth. Seasoned tomatoes, shrimp, chicken, andouille sausage, Old Bay and paprika swirled its way free from the pot like a genie released from his bottle. Everyone's eyes locked onto the conglomeration of rice and proteins.

John gushed, "I'll have you all know I went to great lengths to get alligator meat for this dish."

"You mean that's not chicken?" balked Carla.

"No ma'am. I had to special order alligator from the Cajun Grocer, fresh farm-raised alligator all the way from Louisiana. Michael wouldn't have had me prepare this dish any other way if he were here." There was no mistaking the sadness in John's tone as he reminisced about his partner.

"Here's to Michael," called out Jeremiah raising his frothy glass of homemade brew. Everyone raised their glass, echoing the sentiment. John shared the highlights of his jambalaya preparation, explaining his recipe began with the traditional method of sautéing the "holy trinity."

"What's the 'holy trinity'?" Shelly asked.

"It's the base used in many Southern dishes," answered Rose, "a combination of diced carrots, onion and green bell pepper."

"You're more familiar with the French version, *mire poix*" added Kyle, "which is carrots, onion and celery."

"Oh yes, okay. Wonder why I'd never heard that before," replied Shelly, her voice trailing off as she tilted her head.

John went on to tell the group he had used a mixture of olive oil and butter while sautéing to derive flavor from the butter while increasing the smoking point with the olive oil.

"Here's something else you might not know." John continued. "Back in the day, jambalaya was prepared outdoors in huge black iron pots that were also used for boiling sugar cane syrup. The permanent coating on the interior of the cooking vessels only served to impart an earthy sweetness to the savored flavor of the jambalaya."

"So did you go the extra mile John and coat your pot with syrup?" teased Jim.

"No, but that's not a bad idea for next time," mused John. He went on to share the pots were so large and oversized, brimming with such huge amounts of jambalaya that boat paddles were said to be used for stirring.

"Wonder if those paddles didn't impart their own river flavor," commented Kyle.

"I don't suppose they bothered to clean the boat paddles before using them to stir the food," murmured Rose.

"Well, if they didn't, that only means the paddles were extremely well seasoned," chimed in Carla.

"I'm not worried about bacteria or splinters from paddles, Rose," answered Jim. "My only worry is whether you will get enough of this rapturous rice, meat and vegetable combo after I fill my plate."

Patrice and Maureen were up next in unveiling their individual side dishes. Both women had prepared items featuring green beans in the lead roles, yet the costumes, designs and flavors of each side dish were uniquely different. Maureen prepared her green beans by simply boiling them just to the point of being ever-so-tender. Then she plunged the beans, also known as "string," "pole," "snap" or "zydeco" into an ice bath. The ice bath stops the carryover cooking and helps to maintain the vibrant green color of the vegetable. Maureen explained how after the ice shock she immediately tossed the bright green pods into a sauté pan heated with a bit of olive oil along with some minced onion and garlic. A handful of fresh chopped rosemary and Italian parsley were next, then just a pinch of cayenne pepper and salt. Maureen ended up with a pretentious and frank version of this high-in-Vitamin-A-and-C vegetable.

"Carla, you and I are going to love these bean dishes. I can just tell!" announced Gilda.

Patrice drew back the curtain of her one act play of the starring green bean. Hers wore French costuming (consistent with the French Cajun-Creole theme). *"Haricot vert*! The French word for green bean", announced Patrice as she lifted the tightly wrapped foil cover from the casserole dish. The French beans are sliced length wise, as opposed to across like those we usually see in our American markets. Her beans were joined by a cast of characters which included baby artichoke hearts, "I cooked and extracted these chokes from fresh artichokes this morning, I'll have you know," she revealed, garlic, crumbles of bleu cheese, raisins and smoked almonds. This cast of players came together dressed and ready for baking until they were considered well acquainted with their individual flavors intertwined.

Gilda offered the meal a complimentary accent with a myriad of flavors in her salad of bitter greens, crisp radishes and heirloom tomatoes, intended to offset the richness of the other dishes. Her abundantly filled wooden bowl of this compound salad was set right next to Patrice's Tabasco cheddar biscuits. These rustic and rather spikey-looking, golden brown puffs had so much zest and heat it's likely the biscuits themselves were glad to be sitting next to Gilda's bowl of fresh, cooling greens.

But the absolute star of the show, as agreed upon by all the Friends Amid Food, definitely was Jimmy's Shrimp & Duck Sausage Gumbo. This dish exemplified Jim's willingness to live and play outside the box, to take risks with foods by shopping in exotic and ethnic markets searching out ingredients most home cooks only read about.

This pourer of concrete, painter of watercolors, master of gardeners created an incredible tribute to the culinary traditions of Spain and France that emerged from the Bayou known as "gumbo!" Jim explained to all members present, as they stood by in wild anticipation, that gumbo allows for plenty of artistic license and makes excellent use of leftover proteins. Jim reminded his guests about his feelings on wasting perfectly good food as he nodded towards Rose, instructing her to begin mounding the sticky, white rice steaming in another pot on the stove, into individual bowls.

Jim spoke emphatically as he addressed his guests. "You are free to use whatever pleases you in your own gumbo, but two things are an absolute must: First, a good roux, light golden to a dark, nutty brown in color, it's your choice. I like to take mine to the dark, nutty brown stage. Second, the "holy trinity."

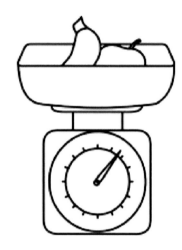

"Yes, the hoooly trinity." John repeated, shaking his hands up over his head and sounding like a preacher praising the gospel of good food.

The Friends stood in line holding their bowlfuls of rice at the ready as Jim dramatically began to ladle spoonfuls of the long-awaited gumbo into each bowl. He continued, raving about the marvel of ingredients that comprised real gumbo.

"First, I start by whisking together my roux, which as you all know is an equal mixture of fat and flour. I usually use a combination of unsalted butter and some pork fat with my flour.

"Of course you do," smiled Diana.

"Before I really got the hang of preparing this dish, I kept making little mistakes. More than I few times I used too much pork fat."

"Jim, Jim", taunted Jeremiah shaking his head, "there's no such thing as too much pork fat."

"True, my friend, so true. Other times I'd walk away and let my roux cook too long. My roux would go beyond white, which is the first color of roux, past level two, blond, then suddenly it would cook past a nice golden brown, and I'd look into the pot to find it was over-cooked, looking more like cinnamon mixed with chocolate. A roux that dark would ruin the gumbo in my opinion. It would have a burnt overtone." Jim instructed his food companions, "If you go beyond that golden brown-nutty hue, it's best to just throw the mixture out and start over." Jim continued to serve heaping amounts of gumbo as he talked. Once his roux achieved the perfect hue, Jim added only half of his holy trinity. He said this was a little secret he learned a few years ago. "Adding the trinity in two separate batches helps to stop the cooking of that roux, so you don't inadvertently take it too far."

By now, more than a few Friends had stopped listening to Jim as they already received their helpings of rice and gumbo. They were huddled over, busy consuming and savoring, eyes glazed. The others remained obediently standing in line, wearing pleading expressions on their faces as though they were the orphaned children in Oliver Twist who asked, "Please, sir, may I have some more?"

Jim went on to tell his guests he then added one full bottle of Abita, the amber lager beer Jeremiah had suggested. Next, five cloves of freshly minced garlic are added along with a generous handful of flat parsley.

Everyone knew without doubt, Jim had artistically chopped the parsley with one of his favorite kitchen tools, the mezzaluna. More seasonings follow dried oregano and thyme, cayenne and Creole, the remaining half of the trinity, and some Crystal Hot Sauce, of course, salt and pepper to taste. Then came the duck sausage Jim had broiled earlier (that's what had been cooking in his Viking oven when they arrived), lots of sausage and lots of shrimp. "A total three pounds of meat," Jim announced the quantity with authority. He then brought it all together with a combination of both shrimp and chicken stock. "The finishing touch filé," Jim said. As Jim began to serve himself, the others peered up from their bowls nodding as if to say "aaahhh, yes . . . the filé," but no one actually said it as their mouths were full of this duck sausage and shrimp utopia.

Patrice, Carla and Gilda watched their meat-eating friends, some sitting, some still standing as they shoveled the glorious gumbo into their giddy mouths. Though Gilda was already beginning to feel full, she was not a vegetarian. "I gotta try a taste," Gilda stated.

Forgoing the rice, she was completely satisfied spooning a small amount of the flavorful broth along with a bit of chicken and sausage from the serving pot directly into her mouth. No one but Rose noticed. Jeremiah, whose eyes were still closed as he was so enraptured in the layers of flavor and taste of Jim's gumbo, barely noticed when his wife Nina, who was finally able to attend this time, wiped away the droplets of broth from his beard.

This dish was definitely worth waiting for. With everyone now assembled around the table and the various Cajun and Creole dishes heaped onto their plates the Friends ate and ate and ate. A satisfying ninety, or so, minutes later, all the savory foods had been consumed with deep appreciation and gusto. It was obvious to everyone a pause in dining was required.

The break continued as conversations ensued and the sipping of beer and wine resumed. After sufficient time had passed, when they felt they would truly enjoy their just desserts, the curtain was lifted for the second act of this dramatic yet ebullient dining experience.

When she had arrived at the start of the party Diana carried a beautifully woven basket lined with gingham linen and filled with her cellophane-wrapped homemade pralines. Diana used a tried and true recipe she'd gotten from her book *The Commander's Palace New Orleans Cookbook*, 1984. An avid collector of cookbooks for years, her collection has gone from grand to magnificent to full library status. Diana has been interviewed and photographed in several news articles as her collection of cookbooks and cook's magazines is so impressive and extensive.

While the recipe she used really didn't need any adaptations or corrections, Diana made the very best version possible. She accomplished this by opting out of just going to the local grocery market to purchase her ingredients. Specifically, for the pecans required to make the candy, Diana told her friends she used pecans she had special-ordered from one of her favorite purveyors of nuts in California.

"Here, taste the pecans. I brought a few here for you all to try," exclaimed Diana.

"Wow. Okay, these have got to be the Chardonnay of pecans!" oozed Rose.

Diana's Southern pralines were cooked exactly to the soft-ball stage preventing any gritty texture to these Naw'lins treats. Her culinary knowledge and proclivity for perfection always result in reliable rewards and tastes for those smart enough to include her at their tables.

Jonah and Colin, also consistent in their choice and preparation of dishes, hit another homerun. When these boys had entered the house, the aroma of their dish preceded them. They're offering for the evening was a lusty bread pudding with whisky sauce, another traditional Southern treat. Jonah initially expressed concern about the texture and taste of their preparation.

"You know, this is the first time I've made bread pudding or whisky sauce," Jonah sounded almost apologetic.

"Don't fret, Jonah, that's one of the reasons we have supper club," Diana reminded him, "so we can try out new recipes on each other and give feedback. Now feed us so we can give you some feedback."

"It looks wonderful guys, but I'm afraid I'm going to have to abstain," said Carla gloomily.

"Me too. Well, I can't have the bread pudding, but I can taste the sauce," replied Gilda, again spooning from the serving pot into her mouth.

As Nina helped with the warming and stirring of the whiskey sauce, Jonah dusted the filled ramekins of bread pudding with powdered sugar. The sauce was sublime, echoing some of the ingredients from the pudding itself - heavy cream, whole milk, white sugar, butter and corn syrup with the addition of a dark, smooth bourbon. The pudding was a magnificent show of how to put to good use crusty day-old bread, farm fresh eggs (from a customer at their store) brown sugar, vanilla, cinnamon, pecans and raisins.

"Jonah, your worries were unfounded. This pudding is an amalgam of excellent taste and texture," exclaimed Nina, as she licked the back of her bourbon anglaise coated spoon.

Meanwhile, Shelly had adorned the dessert table with her take on trifle. She used pound cake rather than lady fingers, introducing coconut amid a mixture of fresh berries and custard instead of jam. And best of all, in Colin's mind, Shelly omitted the sherry the traditional liquor used to make this drunken dessert, and used the established southern comfort, bourbon. "Bourbon instead of sherry, in keeping with the Naw'lins theme," said Shelly.

There was also an attempt to one other New Orleans dessert, bananas foster. While all the right ingredients were on hand the bananas, the butter, the brown sugar and yes, the almost by now redundant bourbon - the flame was not. No matter how many times she tried, Rose couldn't get the dish to burst into flames.

"Why isn't it igniting?" asked Gilda. "Is it because the banana liqueur is missing?"

"No, that shouldn't be the problem, she added the bourbon which is higher in proof than banana liqueur, so it should be lighting up," answered John.

Diana suggested the flame may have failed because Rose was using a nonstick pan rather than a heavy cast iron skillet. No matter, flame or no flame, the wow factor was in the taste not their eyes this time. The Friends ate it anyway.

In spite of the bananas failing to "foster" this was another tribute to the Friends Amid Food and their commitment to all that is delectable in the world of food fodder. As usual, there was as much fun as there was learning and sharing. Their palates were saturated and their food spirits embraced. Now it was time to go home and sleep it off. Until next month.

Shrimp Po'boys With Spicy Aioli

Ingredients:

1 pound shrimp - peeled and deveined

1½ cups cornmeal

1 tablespoon garlic powder

1 teaspoon salt

2 tablespoons olive oil

1/4 cup mayonnaise

Dash of your favorite red hot sauce

2 small French or Hoagie rolls

1 large beef steak tomato - sliced

1½ cups all-purpose flour

3 tablespoons Creole seasoning

1 tablespoon paprika

3/4 teaspoon cayenne pepper

4 tablespoons unsalted butter

1 large clove garlic - minced

1 tablespoon horseradish

2-3 leaves iceberg lettuce - shredded

1 large dill pickle - thinly sliced

Preparation:

1) In shallow pan combine flour, cornmeal, Creole seasoning, garlic powder, paprika and salt.

2) Heat oil and butter in heavy skillet.

3) Dredge peeled, deveined shrimp in flour mixture and sauté in skillet until no longer white/gray but pinkish/white in color. You may have to cook the shrimp in 2 or 3 batches to avoid overcrowding the pan.

4) While shrimp are cooking, prepare aioli; by combining mayonnaise, minced garlic, red hot sauce, cayenne pepper and horseradish in small mixing bowl.

5) When all shrimp have been cooked prepare sandwiches by slicing the two rolls in half length-wise then brush both sides of the interior of each roll with the spicy aioli (as you would when preparing a sandwich).

6) Pile shrimp onto one side of each half then top with shredded lettuce, pickles and tomato slices.

7) Cut each sandwich in half - serve with quarter of lemon as garnish for each sandwich half.

Note: For those opting out of eating bread, shrimp can be served on a large lettuce leaf with a slice of tomato and a pickle on the side.

Makes four 4-ounce servings

Haricot Vert with Artichokes

Ingredients:

1 pound haricot verts - cleaned and ends trimmed (if using standard green beans, after cleaning and trimming, slice the beans lengthwise to mimic haricot verts)

1/4 cup unsalted butter

Pinch cayenne pepper

3 cloves fresh garlic - minced

1/4 cup crumbled bleu cheese

1/4 teaspoon fresh rosemary - minced

3/4 teaspoon kosher salt

1/4 cup fresh parsley - minced

large bowl of ice water

1 small red onion - thinly sliced in rounds

1 package frozen artichoke hearts - quartered and thawed

Preparation:

1) In a large saucepot, bring salted water to a boil.

2) Add beans - cover and cook for 5-7 minutes.

3) Immediately strain water out of saucepot and plunge beans into a bowl of ice water to stop the cooking.

4) Using the same saucepot, heat butter over medium heat - add sliced onions and sauté until onions are fragrant and translucent.

5) Add minced garlic and cook another 3 minutes.

6) Add artichoke hearts and cook another 3 minutes.

7) Return cooled beans to saucepot and gently stir in rosemary, parsley and cayenne pepper.

8) Cook just until beans are heated through - season to taste with salt and pepper.

Makes eight 4-ounce servings

Shrimp and Duck Sausage Gumbo

Ingredients:

1 bottle of Abita beer or other amber lager

Crystal Hot Sauce or other sauce of your choice

1 pound shrimp - shelled and deveined

4-5 cloves fresh garlic - minced

1-2 tablespoons Worcestershire sauce

1 tablespoon filé powder

Cooked white rice - enough to yield 12 4-oz servings

1 large green bell pepper - seeds and ribs removed - small diced

1 pound duck sausage - if unable to find, substitute andouille sausage - cut into 1/4 inch slices and cooked through

1 quart chicken or vegetable stock

1/2 cup all-purpose flour

2 stalks celery - small diced

1/2 cup peanut oil

1 medium onion - diced

1 tablespoon Cajun seasoning

Salt and pepper to taste

Preparation:

1) Prepare your roux by heating the oil in a large, heavy Dutch oven or cast iron pot. Whisk in flour and stir constantly over medium-low heat until mixture thickens and reaches a dark blond, but not too dark, hue – similar in color to peanut butter. About 16-21 minutes.

2) Mix in the "holy trinity," onion, bell pepper and celery, cooking for about 5-7 minutes, until vegetables have softened.

3) Add minced garlic, cooking another 5 minutes.

4) Slowly begin to ladle in warm stock/beer mixture into vegetables, lowering the heart and simmering for 30 minutes.

5) Stir in duck sausage and Worcestershire sauce, simmering another 5 minutes.

6) Add shrimp and cook 3-5 minutes, until shrimp are soft pink in color.

7) Gently stir in Cajun seasoning, along with salt and pepper to taste.

8) When ready to serve, place 2-3 ounces of rice in individual serving bowls and top each with 1-2 ounces of gumbo mixture.

9) Garnish each serving with a pinch of filé powder and a dash or two of hot sauce.

Makes twelve 4-ounce servings

Bananas Foster

Ingredients:

1/2 cup firmly packed dark brown sugar

1/4 teaspoon ground cinnamon

4 ripe, yet firm bananas - split and quartered

1/2 cup walnut bits

1/4 cup unsalted butter

1/4 cup banana liqueur or brandy

1/3 cup rum

ice cream - French vanilla or praline

Preparation:

1) In a large heavy skillet combine brown sugar, butter and cinnamon over medium-low heat, stirring constantly with a wooden spoon or silicone spatula until mixture begins to bubble.

2) Carefully place sliced bananas and liqueur or brandy into skillet - cook until bananas soften - about 2-3 minutes.

3) Tilting the skillet away from you – pour all the rum into pan. The fumes from the alcohol and gas flame will ignite the rum as you tilt the pan. If you're a little nervous, you can lift and remove the skillet from your burner, pour in the rum and use an extended barbeque lighter to ignite the rum. In both cases, always hold the pan away from your face and body.

4) When the flames subside, remove banana slices from the skillet and evenly distribute among 8 dessert bowls. Place one small scoop of ice cream in the center and spoon remaining in skillet over each serving.

5) Generously garnish each bowl with walnut bits.

Makes eight 4-ounce servings

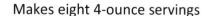

Sweet and Savory, Deep Dish and Rustic - May

"Milk Flabby!" No we're not talking thighs. "French Silk." Are we referring to Sophie's complexion? "Whoopie." Well, Ray Charles makes reference to it in one of his songs, but this isn't that kind of whoopie. "Shoo-fly!" No, we're not picnicking at the moment either. If you haven't figured it out yet, we're talking pies! Raisin, custard, lemon meringue, Boston cream, meat, onion, egg, and of course, fruit. *Pâte à choux*, basic, cookie, graham or puff are just a few of the options available for a tasty foundation or lattice topping for those fillings that urge one to delve into the depths of the porcelain, or in some cases aluminum, spheres beckoning from the pastry shop windows - or if you're lucky, your mother's cooling rack.

It was spring time and Diana and her husband Stanley had offered to host the Friends Amid Food May gathering. There was a moment when she had paused and reconsidered her "pies" theme, since there were one or two responses to her invitation that pies would make a more suitable food theme in fall or winter.

"*Au contrairé!*" rebutted Maureen via email. And without hesitation, she encouraged Diana and Stanley to stick to their pie theme with the velocity of caramel topping on a warm oatmeal and brown sugar coated apple crisp. "Lest we all forget there are quiches and tarts, oversized-deep dish to small individual, sweet boysenberry and cherry to savory meat and cheese. A pie can be sinfully rich or elegantly light."

The options Maureen had spun in the minds of her Friends were without limits. Before they knew it, those apprehensive supper club members had warmed to the pie theme. Discussions were bantered about in emails and phone conversations more so than other previous dinner themes. Apparently there are some emotional ties connected to the idea of pie making. Once the idea took hold, more than a couple of the Friends claimed "dibs" on their favorite pies, many connected to memories of holiday gatherings or recipes passed down from family members. Even Gilda could picture in her mind's eye her great aunt's peach crostada bubbling hot in a glass Pyrex pie dish and cooling on a bunched up red and white gingham dish towel.

Including recollections of holiday celebrations where, "What kind of pie do you want?" being shouted from the kitchen, followed by responses like, "One slice of each!" replied in chorus by those waiting at the dining table.

While some supper club members embraced the opportunity to try out something new in the art of pie making, others knew veering from tradition can be near sacrilegious. Such is the case with Rose's pumpkin pie from scratch. Ever since she went the extra mile one Thanksgiving by seasoning and roasting a fresh whole pumpkin, the use of canned puree has been shunned by every one of her family members. This supper club menu spurred a couple members to create new twists in a realm of familiarity.

Finally, that first Sunday in May arrived, and one by one our group of foodies began to ring the doorbell of Diana and Stanley's home. Diana and Stanley are well-versed as gracious hosts due to the many number and style of parties they have given over the years, ranging from pig roasts to formal sit-downs, high teas, barbeques and cocktail. Their guest lists have included celebrity chefs and city mayors, next-door neighbors, family members from far away and close friends. Tonight the Friends Amid Food are considered family. Stanley greeted each member with a warm hug and a choice of red or white wine from his extensive and much-envied wine collection. As the kitchen filled with food and friends, the sound of glasses clinking together in personalized and congratulatory toasts rang through the room. It never fails; every supper club gathering feels at once new and exciting yet gives everyone a sense of coming home to warmth and comfort.

It has only been six weeks since their last dinner but the recent change in season from scorching summer heat to slightly cooler spring waved in alterations among the lives of many of the Friends.

Maureen shared she had finally grown more comfortable in her new job. A feeling she was not sure would ever come about. Still she complained that while many of her co-workers were as cerebral as she, none among them appeared to have any real interest in food.

Rose's youngest son had decided to join the Army. She shared her own surprise that the "old hippie" in her was not so dismayed about his decision after all. "Considering his recent shenanigans over the last few months, it might be good for him," she mused. What Rose didn't share out loud was her concern about those freeze-dried food rations her son would be destined to live on.

Diana had been considering Colin's offer to teach cooking classes at the culinary shop he and Jonah own, as they had discussed expanding the store to add a small demonstration kitchen. Patrice announced she was now open to any and all adult interaction whenever possible between diaper changes, bath time and baby playtime. Sophie and Kyle quietly exhibited their consistent demeanor of calm and amusement as they moved from one conversation to the next, remaining attached to one another's hips. After an hour or so of conversation and catching up, Diana pulled the last pie from the oven while giving the cue to the others the food introductions were to begin shortly.

Gilda hurried over to the large dining table knowing these introductions should not be missed. She had always favored pies over cake. As everyone completed the assembly of their baked goods on the immense dining table, Gilda announced, "If you all don't mind, I would love to emcee tonight."

"Gilda, Diana and Stanley are our hosts tonight. It's their turn to be ring masters over tonight's food event," chided Rose.

"Oh we don't mind," replied Diana. "You go right ahead Miss Gilda."

Setting her water bottle to the side, Gilda asked Jimmy to kick off the evening by describing the deep-dish pie that steamed on the table directly in front of him. Jim exhibited his knowledge of all that is based in culinary and brew by sharing the origin of the beer he used in his pie, Guinness Stout. According to Jim, Guinness saw its beginning in the brewery of Arthur Guinness at St. James Gate in Ireland.

"Guinness," Jim informed his audience, "is a direct descendent of the Porter style of beer which originated in London in the early 1800's."

"I'm not sure what Porter style beer is, are you?" Gilda whispered to Sophie. Sophie shook her head.

"Porter is a dark beer made from brown malt. Back in the day, they used the term Extra Porter, Double Porter or Stout Porter to describe those Porters that were stronger than usual. The name then was shortened to Stout. Now Guinness", Jim continued as he winked at Gilda, "has a more robust and coffee flavor to its tone, some say burnt. At one time there was even some controversy about the Guinness brewing practice of blending portions of the aged brew with the fresh brew to create the unique sharp and tangy lactic flavor. But this has been denied by the brewers of Guinness."

"What about the bubbles floating downward? Tell us about the bubbles," interjected Stanley.

"Well, I'm glad you brought that up," replied Jim with a Cheshire cat grin. This question is one he had hoped would be asked since he had long ago researched this phenomenon. "It's the combination of nitrogen and CO_2 along with the use of widgets in the canned versions of Guinness

along with the deep color of the beer in contrast to the light caramel color of the head all contribute to the 'appearance' of the bubbles floating downward. As you pour the brew into the tulip shaped glass it cascades down and the bubbles begin bumping their way against the side of the glass. This beer is best served in the tall tulip glasses and that's what makes this work. The bubbles immediately float back up in the center creating a column which goes mostly undetected in the dark colored beer. What we see, are those bubbles making their way down the sides of the glass, giving Guinness the unique reputation as the beer with bubbles that float down instead of up!" Everyone was duly impressed.

"Besides the Guinness, what else is in your pie?" inquired Diana.

"Oh, that would be . . .," Jim paused and took another languid sip from his beer, "pork."

"Yes," were the murmurings from the Friends. "Of course pork." Everyone was keenly aware of Jim's long standing love affair with pork. "Along with potatoes, onions and mushrooms, it doesn't get better than that," Jim added. He was right, this deep-dish pie was an experience in the very basics of a good food foundation. Beginning with straight forward, grown in the best of soil vegetables mixed with richly fed pigs and a simply seasoned Guinness based beef broth, created a wholesome, hearty taste. This was a real man's pie.

Next up was Colin (Jonah was still at his baseball game and would arrive later). Colin began to describe the laborious task of making each of the individual tartlets he and Jonah prepared earlier in the day by first preparing a basic pie dough. From there he detailed how they caramelized the white onions, leeks and the aromatic shallot in a combination of olive oil, unsalted butter and sherry with fresh thyme added at the very end. The tartlets were then finished off in the oven to create that signature puffy, golden crust that supported the sweetened onions and the soft, silky melted gruyere cheese.   Only a handful of ingredients were used for these small but delectable treasures. And they were treasures. Still standing around the dining table the Friends popped these little tartlets as though they had been medicinally prescribed not even waiting for them to be properly plated.

"So Colin you and Jonah made onion tartlets and Patrice prepared an entire onion pie?" Gilda asked before she made the next food introduction.

"Yup and they're very different," piped Patrice, "because I used Bryant's French onion soup recipe as the base for my pie.   Remember?   He uses the vegetarian Worcestershire sauce which is actually deeper in color than beef broth. The boys used onion but also leeks, which are not in my pie, or the soup for that matter."   Those who attended the French vegetarian supper club and were privileged to consume Chef's French onion soup knew what they had to look forward to in Patrice's pie.

"Yes, that and the fact that Byrant takes his onions further than is commonly directed in most recipes, caramelizing them ever so slowly over low heat for an extended time," Rose added.

"She's right. I've learned to watch and wait as the onions begin to sweat, then change color like autumn leaves going from light golden, pliable tendrils to dark coffee bean brown semicircles. Sweet and crispy and just on the very verge of burnt," Patrice explained.

Bryant taught Patrice to allow nature's underground bulbs, which happen to be related to lilies, to transform themselves to the point where they gleefully exuded a concentration of their natural sugar thereby adding a depth of flavor often missed in other onion soups. His are cooked with a dark roux creating a kind of onion saltwater taffy of confection. This gave Patrice's pie filling a luxurious pigment before the baking even began. Indeed, when the Friends had finally sat down to eat, her French onion pie was a reminder that if we are patient and poised at the stove we come away with a dish that is multifaceted in flavor.

With the memory of a past experience far enough behind her, Gilda was able to smile as Rose stepped forward to introduce the Cornish pasties she had fine-tuned to suit Gilda's palate and stomach capacity for pastries. A few Friends already knew the story of when Rose and Gilda were in London and went to visit an English Pub where they learned how the English pasty came about. Their origin was of convenience which is often the case for how wonderful foods come into being. Pasties were simply a method of using up leftovers from the previous evening's dinner. English wives would combine the small remaining amount of meat, lamb or beef (likely a tough cut that had been boiled and cooked until fork-tender) along with potatoes, carrots and onions. Early the next morning she would rise and prepare a basic pie dough cutting rounds about eight to ten inches in diameter. Using her food mill, the lady of the house would mill and mix together the meat and vegetables into a well-blended purée. Then she would spoon the mixture onto one side of the pastry round finally topping the mixture off with only a bit of gravy or drippings. Next she would fold the other side over creating a crescent shape, pinching the edges closed with a fork and pop the turnovers into the oven.

A hearty but easy to pack meal was created for her husband who likely worked long hours in the tin mines of Cornwall.

"Now I follow the same method of preparation except I include a variety of seasonings and fresh herbs to a better cut of beef, with very small diced potatoes, carrots and onions. For enhanced flavor my filling includes mushrooms and shallots. Since Sis can only eat about four ounce portions, I keep my pasties six inches in diameter," Rose explained during her food introduction. "For eye appeal I of course brush the pastry with an egg wash before placing into the oven, giving, as you can see, a beautiful golden hue to my version of this utilitarian meat pie."

"Rosie's version offers more intrigue and interest than any we ate in London. I love 'em. But still, I can usually only eat one, but it's always a good one," chirped Gilda.

"Okay next is Sophie and Kyle. Introduce us to your pie please," encouraged Gilda.

"Ours is another pie of savory tradition, but American tradition - chicken pot pie," Kyle responded.

"This pie was prepared with lots of love and care," beamed Sophie. Kyle and Sophie took turns explaining the combination of flavorsome ingredients that cozied up and nestled together in a near cavernous vintage pie dish, bathed in a rich country chicken gravy. Sophie explained the simplicity of her approach to this family favorite. "I of course, begin with a freshly prepared herb-roasted chicken. You can use the commercially prepared chickens at the grocery store, but making one fresh, really makes a difference. My grandmother would roll over in her grave if I ever used one of those."

"She's right. I was there when one time, she used a ready-cooked chicken in this pie, and both her parents made a face at the table," Kyle shared. Sophie went on to explain after cooling enough to handle, the chicken was shredded, the russet potatoes, onion and sweet carrots were small diced to accommodate small bites and sautéed in a mixture of unsalted butter and olive oil. Then the herb-roasted chicken is combined with vegetables and are joined together in a deep round casserole dish that has been lined with a buttery pastry crust. The filling is then topped with another layer of this same pastry. Those familiar slits are cut into the pastry top allowing steam to release and prevent the filling from bursting through.

"They also allow us to breathe in that aroma of comfort most people associate with home-cooking, mom, dad and a Chrysler in the driveway," boomed Jim. "Sophie your chicken pot pie looks like it should be in Norman Rockwell painting."

"I gotta tell you Sophie, if Mr. Rockwell were here with us to enjoy your chicken pot pie, I'd say Jimmy is right, a half-eaten depiction of your pie would end up in one of his paintings!" declared Jonah as he entered the dining room, trailing bits of dust and dirt behind him as if he were the Peanuts character Pig-Pen coming in from a baseball game.

"Well it looks really good Soph, but with all that crust I have to be happy with tasting just one bite of the filling," pouted Gilda.

"Well, that's the best part," chimed in Kyle.

Diana prepared two pies, one sweet, one savory. Her savory pie was a rectangular tart of cheeses, heirloom tomatoes, and fresh basil all atop a flaky crust. For those who enjoy Caprese salad or even better, seasoned, roasted beefsteak tomatoes topped with a mixture of grated Parmesan and Asiago cheeses and a sprinkling of fresh basil chiffonade, then you've had Diana's tart minus her

perfect crust. This rectangular tart added visual interest to the table with Diana's use of colorful heirlooms and it was not round in shape as were the other offerings.

The weather, as always during supper club gatherings, was in cooperation with the event allowing everyone to balance their platefuls with beverage of choice and venture out to select a seat on the back patio. All conversations came to a momentary halt as the Friends savored the sampling of pies. By the end of the better part of an hour not a single dinner pie was left uneaten.

As the sun began to dip down, Jim offered each Friend a sampling of his dessert beer, his newest brew was a sweet full bodied blend of dark berries and chocolate.

"Berries and chocolate in beer?" asked Kyle incredulously.

"Yes, beer that includes cherries and chocolate in the brewing process. It is fabulous! Even for you non-beer drinkers over there, Rose and Gilda," exuded Jim.

This new taste fandango injected excitement and enthusiasm and renewed conversations and questions about micro-brews and the overall development of beer since its football and lawn mowing days. The result brought everyone to their feet and back to the dining table inside ready to indulge in the selection of dessert pies.

Sophie kept to her theme of family favorites by preparing a bright lemon custard topped high with a most exquisite meringue, white and fluffy with ombre tips baked to a light golden brown. Diana was more multicultural in her pie preparation. Italian for her dinner pie, then French for her dessert pie expressed with an apple tartin. The crust was perfect in taste and texture. Anything less from her and the Friends would have been genuinely shocked and surprised. The crisp tart apples were not hidden under pastry but were left exposed as thinly sliced crescent moons assembled in a concentric pattern and arranged in such an orderly and organized fashion, each apple slice was given an equal share of the cinnamon and sugar mixture.

Rose took a different approach to her dessert pie in that she interplayed sweet with savory. Using a cornmeal crust similar to the one Diana used for her savory pie Rose displayed an artistic installation of honeyed chévre, heavy cream, brown sugar, fresh blueberries and fresh basil. This pie offered the taste buds a heightened experience in flavor layering. The tongue's first impression was that of bright tartness, the lemon, tempered with a soft sweet tanginess, delivered by the chévre. This is followed up with the fresh blueberries that popped lively in your mouth but were cushioned with the rich, heavy cream mixed with dark brown  sugar. Finally, the tongue receives the taste of mint's earthy cousin, basil, all neatly tied together with the crunch of toasted slivered almonds. This created such a cacophony of taste all the Friends had to take a second bite just to see if that sequence of flavors would incite the same oral riot. It did and it was just as pleasing on the third and fourth bites!

"Rosie," Gilda leaned over to her sister whispering, "In case you didn't notice, I've opted out of everyone else's dessert pie, because this is my very favorite dessert of yours."

"I thought my chocolate pudding was your favorite dessert."

"Oh right. Okay, this is my second favorite dessert of yours," admitted Gilda.

It was with whimsy and creativity that Patrice produced her pie pops, small rounds of buttery crust, some filled with pumpkin spiced pie filling, some with apple and others with cherry, all presented on white lollipop sticks and decorated with a drizzling of colored icing depicting the filling inside. Patrice had wrapped each pie pop with cellophane then tied it closed with a ribbon.

"When did you have time to do these?!" asked Rose, obviously impressed.

Patrice could see as she looked around the table that all her Friends expressed awe at her

creation. Everyone agreed, between diaper changes, playtime on the floor, feedings and all the rest that comes with caring for a new baby, Patrice's attention to detail in her presentation that evening was to be applauded.

But the dessert pie that insisted upon being savored and eaten as if in a slow motion film replay was Maureen's bitter sweet chocolate tart. It seems true, for many there are times when finishing an otherwise satisfying meal, there is still a desire to finish off with just a morsel of chocolate. Maureen's chocolate tart was prepared with exactly that feeling in mind. Each Friend was given an oh so thin slice of this deep dark decadence.

"I used Ghirardelli's bitter sweet chocolate for this pie. Then I folded it into a voluptuous mixture of heavy cream and unsalted butter. This pie is a concentration of the very essence of chocolate that just happens to sit atop a very simple and basic pie crust," proclaimed Maureen.

There was nothing fancy or distracting about this tart. Maureen didn't try to recreate the wheel by adding berries or building height, there were no bells, no whistles. Just chocolate as it is meant to be enjoyed. A few Friends allowed Maureen to add a dollop of barely sweetened cream whipped only to the point of soft, yielding peaks. The cream, spooned slightly askew on each slice, was situated in such a way it looked rather like a seductive woman barely balancing herself upon the edge of a gentleman's lap. You find you can't help but notice her and envy him. This was the allure of Maureen's tart, which went amazingly well with Jim's dessert beer.

"I'm going to have a glass of red wine with this tart," squealed Sophie between bites. "Chocolate and red wine go together like peanut butter and jelly or ketchup and fries."

"I agree," reiterated Rose. "Certainly not milk, this is not a child's chocolate pie."

As the sun dipped below the horizon the Friends Amid Food finished their dessert pies in the lighting provided by Diana and Stanley's torch lamps. Carrying empty plates and cups from the patio to the kitchen thank yous and goodbyes were quietly uttered among the group of well-fed Friends. It was indeed a most satisfying meal consisting only of pies and not one morsel left to take home.

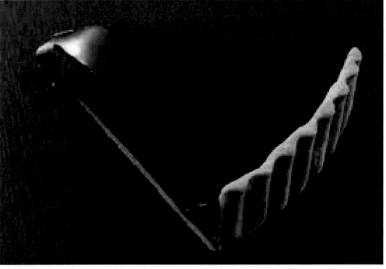

Caramelized Onion and Leek Tart

Ingredients:

5-6 ounces grated Gruyére cheese

2 tablespoons each, unsalted butter and olive oil

1 whole egg beaten with water - for egg wash

1-2 leeks - green parts removed, cleaned and sliced

1 large sweet onion - small diced

2 tablespoons fresh thyme - leaves only

1/4 teaspoon ground black pepper

1 package puff pastry - thawed

1/4 teaspoon kosher salt

1 shallot - minced

1/4 cup sherry

Special Equipment: parchment paper or silpat, two cookie sheets

Preparation: Preheat oven to 400 degrees

1) In a large, heavy skillet over medium heat, warm butter and olive oil.

2) Add sliced onion and cook stirring occasionally for about 30 minutes. Until onions are well caramelized.

3) Add shallot, leeks and sherry to skillet, sautéing until leeks are soft and translucent, another 5-7 minutes. Season with salt and pepper.

4) Meanwhile, gently remove puff pastry from package and place on lightly floured counter. Unfold one of the pastry sheets into interior of rectangular tart pan then run rolling pin flat over the top to cut excess dough from edges. Lightly brush pastry with the egg wash.

5) Carefully spoon onion and leek mixture onto top of pastry dough all the way to the edges, sprinkle top with fresh thyme and grated Gruyere cheese.

6) Bake in preheated oven about 20-25 minutes, or until puff pastry is a light golden brown.

Makes sixteen 4-ounce servings

Chicken Pot Pie

Ingredients for Pie Filling:

1/4 cup unsalted butter plus 1 tablespoon

1-2 cups low-sodium chicken broth

1 Spanish or yellow onion - small diced

1 cup small diced celery

1 large russet potato - peeled and small diced

1 whole roasted chicken - skinned, deboned and shredded

Salt and pepper to taste

1/2 cup all-purpose flour

1 tablespoon olive oil

1 cup small diced carrots

1 cup frozen peas

1/4 cup heavy cream

Ingredients for Cheddar Crust:

3 cups all-purpose flour

3 tablespoons unsalted butter - cut into cubes and chilled

1 cup grated sharp cheddar cheese

2 teaspoons kosher salt

1 cup shortening

4-5 tablespoons iced water

Preparation for Crust:

1) In large mixing bowl or food processor combine flour and salt.

2) Using a fork or pastry blender if using a mixing bowl or pulsing if using food processor, add chilled butter and shortening to flour mixture in 3 separate batches until mixture resembles crumbly sand.

3) While machine is running or between stirrings, add water 1 tablespoon at a time until dough comes together into a ball.

4) Using your hands, knead in the grated cheese.

5) Form dough into two separate discs and wrap in plastic wrap. Place in refrigerator for at least 30 minutes to rest. While dough is resting prepare filling for pie.

Preparation for Filling:

1) In large saucepot over medium heat, warm ¼ cup butter and olive oil.

2) Whisk in flour and continue cooking for about 5 minutes, making a light roux

3) Continue whisking adding 1 cup of the chicken broth and the heavy cream. Simmer on low heat until mixture becomes thick and bubbly. Stir in diced onions, carrots, celery, potatoes and peas. Cook until vegetables are softened but still somewhat firm - about 7 to 10 minutes.

4) Stir in shredded chicken and season to taste with salt and pepper.

To Assemble Pie

1) Remove pie dough from refrigerator and using a small dusting of flour on your board or counter roll dough out each disc into rounds large enough to fit into your pie dish with some overlap - about a 12" round will work for a 9" pan.

2) Place one rolled pie crust into a deep pie pan, crimping the edges then prick a few spots on the bottom to prevent bubbling of your crust and add a few pie beads or dried beans (these will also help to prevent your crust from puffing up) then lightly brush the edges of the crust with egg wash.

3) Bake in preheated oven for only 10-15 minutes, just until crust is slightly cooked. This process is referred to as "blind cooking or baking."

4) Allow baked crust to cool slightly, remove pie weights or beans then fill with chicken, vegetable mixture and top with remaining tablespoon of butter.

5) Roll out other dough disc and place on top of filled pie. Crimp the edges carefully and brush top with egg wash. Cut a few slits into the top crust and bake in preheated oven for 45-55 minutes.

Makes eight 4-ounce servings

Savory Heirloom Tomato Pie on Cornmeal Crust

Ingredients for Crust:

1 cup all-purpose flour

3/4 teaspoon kosher salt

1 stick unsalted butter - cubed and chilled

3/4 cup yellow cornmeal

3 tablespoons goat cheese - chilled

3-4 tablespoons iced water

Ingredients for Filling:

2 tablespoons olive oil

2 pounds heirloom tomatoes

3/4 cup goat cheese

1/4 cup sour cream

3 tablespoons fresh chives - minced

1/4 cup fresh basil - chiffonade

1 large white onion - thinly sliced

salt and pepper to taste

3/4 cup mozzarella cheese - cubed

3 tablespoons seasoned bread crumbs

1 tablespoon fresh thyme leaves

fresh cracked pepper to taste

3 tablespoons fresh Italian parsley - chopped, plus 1 for garnish

Preparation for Crust:

1) Using a food processor, pulse together flour, cornmeal and salt. Add the butter and goat cheese through the feed tube in 3 separate batches. Continue pulsing until mixture resembles crumbly sand.

2) Slowly drizzle the iced water in through the feed tube one tablespoon at a time until dough comes together forming a smooth ball.

3) Turn dough out onto a sheet of plastic wrap and cover completely. Flatten into a thick, round disc. Refrigerate for at least 30 minutes.

4) Once dough has rested, remove plastic wrap and place disc between two sheets of parchment paper that have been lightly dusted with flour.

5) Roll out dough into a 13" round then carefully transfer to a pie pan or tart pan. Pierce bottom with a fork and crimp entire edge of pie. Refrigerate for another 15 minutes.

6) Cover bottom of crust with pie weights or beans and blind bake for 15 minutes. Remove pie weights or beans and bake another 15 minutes until crust is a light golden brown.

7) Set aside and allow to cool.

1) Heat 1 tablespoon of the olive oil in a large skillet. When oil is shimmering add sliced onions, cooking until fragrant. Remove onions from skillet and allow to cool on a separate plate.

2) While onions are cooking, remove core/stems and slice tomatoes. Gently toss them in a colander with about 1 teaspoon of kosher salt. Allow tomatoes to drain in sink for about 15 minutes.

3) In a large mixing bowl, combine goat cheese, mozzarella, sour cream, bread crumbs and 2 tablespoons each chives, parsley, basil and thyme. Season with salt and pepper. Top with reserved sautéed onions.

4) Spread cheese and herb mixture carefully into cooled pie crust. Arrange sliced/drained tomatoes on top and drizzle with remaining tablespoon of olive oil.

5) Bake for about 45 minutes or until tomatoes are slightly browned and pie is bubbling.

6) Garnish with remaining tablespoons of herbs and, if desired, additional goat cheese.

Makes eight 4-ounce servings

Blueberry, Honey-Chévre and Basil Pie

Ingredients for Crust:

1¼ cups King Arthur's all-purpose flour

3 tablespoons yellow cornmeal

1/4 teaspoon kosher salt

6 tablespoons unsalted butter - softened

3 tablespoons granulated sugar

1 large egg yolk

1½ tablespoons heavy cream

1 teaspoon vanilla extract

Ingredients for Filling:

1/2 cup honey-chévre (goat cheese)

1/2 cup heavy cream

1 whole, large egg

1/2 cup dark brown sugar

1/4 cup King Arthur's all-purpose flour

1/8 teaspoon kosher salt

1 tablespoon fresh basil - chiffonade

zest of one lemon

2 cups fresh blueberries - rinsed, stems removed (if using frozen do not let them thaw)

Ingredients for Topping and Garnish:

1 cup sliced almonds - lightly toasted

1/2 cup granulated sugar

1/3 cup unsalted butter - melted

1/4 teaspoon ground cinnamon

1/2 cup sour cream or crème fraiche

1 fresh vanilla bean - split lengthwise

Preparation for the Crust:

1) In a medium mixing bowl whisk together flour, cornmeal and salt. Set aside.

2) Using large bowl of your stand mixer, beat butter and sugar together until light in color and fluffy.

3) In a small mixing bowl whisk together egg yolk, heavy cream and vanilla extract. Add this egg and milk mixture to the flour/cornmeal mixture in 2 batches, until mixture comes together in a ball.

4) Using your hands, remove pie dough and place on a large sheet of plastic wrap. Flatten ball into a large disc and chill, completely wrapped in plastic, in refrigerator for at least 30 minutes.

Preparation for Filling:

While dough is resting, using a large mixing bowl and wooden spoon, combine the honey-chévre cheese, heavy cream, egg, brown sugar, flour, salt, fresh basil and lemon zest. Gently fold in blueberries. Set aside until ready to fill crust.

Preparation for Topping and Garnish

1) Lightly toast almonds in a dry, clean skillet over medium heat. Don't walk away, as these can burn quickly. Spoon toasted almonds into a small bowl and stir in sugar and melted butter. Set aside.

2) For the garnish, in a separate small bowl combine sour cream or crème fraiche, using the tip of a small knife scrape bean paste from inside of vanilla bean and add to sour cream. Stir in brown sugar and cinnamon. Set bowl aside.

To Assemble Pie

1) Roll out dough on a lightly floured board or counter. Carefully place in a 9"-10" deep dish pie pan.

2) Pour blueberry mixture over crust.

3) Top with almond mixture and bake in preheated oven for 25 minutes.

4) Allow pie to cool completely then garnish in center or on individual slices with sour cream garnish.

Makes ten 4-ounce servings

Cooks and Gardeners - June

There have been countless occasions when I have witnessed Rose purposely select the weakest and most desperate looking of herbs, plants and flowers when visiting nurseries together. "Why are you picking that one?" I've asked. "I'm taking it home," she says, not taking her eyes from the hapless plant before her. "I'm taking it home to save it," is her most common reply. Thoughts of Charlie Brown and his pathetic Christmas tree and Rose with her near-dead flora has brought me to my inorganic knees in hysterics then later genuine awe as the once scraggly and pathetic grows into lush and fruitful.

I was dealing with some personal difficulties when Rose and Gilda called to invite me to a very special and rather intimate dinner. By now I don't need to tell you how incredible the food was. The profusion of aromas, tastes and textures I experienced in a simple meal comprised only of appetizers brought about a marked shift in my mood and perspective that day. As the summer evening wore on and I continued to munch, savor and consume, I felt as though the food was simultaneously cloaking my doubt and worries while allowing my optimism and hope to rise to the surface like the bubbles of the almond flavored champagne we sipped.

I knew the company I was enjoying accounted in large part to my change in disposition, but I had asked, more to myself than anyone, what was it about this particular meal that seemed to give me clarity of mind while moving me away from the horrible oppression I had felt for weeks?

"The herbs, Kevin," Gilda quietly demurred somehow reading my thoughts. "It's Rose's intentional use of very specific herbs that bring about chemical changes in our minds and bodies. She's been researching it. According to Rosie, plants heal."

I asked Rose what was it exactly about her and her herbs these days. When I had known her in college, Rose was more a mistress of "dry arrangements" than the herbalist and master gardener who was currently flitting around the kitchen. Now she was a ward of nature. Rose paused, looked at me intently, inhaled deeply and tilted her head slightly.

Then she mused, "There are so many reasons why I love cooking with herbs. To begin, they are healthy, natural, of course and multidimensional. In my opinion herbs are best when used fresh, but dried they can offer a more definitive and concentrated addition to food. Herbs are grounded in the earth, giving us the same energy when we consume them and while many herbs are delicate, this grounding gives them strength in their medical properties, which we benefit from. For me, it's as though they're standing in the Mountain pose of yoga, a posture of strength. And just like people, some herbs are subtle in taste while others pack a powerful punch. I love the variety and choices, all the different shapes, sizes, textures, styles and designs herbs come in. I would love to have an herb garden so big and so varied that when I walked out to pick from or tend to my herb garden, it would be as though I were walking into a huge outdoor wardrobe with racks and racks of designer herbs from all over the world. Just imagine it."

Rose went on, speaking more to herself than us. "Cooking with herbs is what sets my food apart. At least I think so."

"No, we all think so Rosie," agreed Gilda as she walked past carrying a platter of something that smelled so lovely I turned my head and watched her walk back out of the kitchen.

Rose babbled on, "I love learning more and more about how to plant, grow and use herbs. There is so much to know. I am so hungry to gain even more knowledge of herbs. It makes me feel somehow closer to nature. And I love that the use of herbs is as old as . . . dirt. You have to respect, Kevin . . . Kevin!" I had momentarily turned all the way around as Gilda walked past again, this time carrying a bowl of fragrant roasted olives, Rose brought me back to her dissertation on herbs. "You gotta respect the long-recorded uses of herbs for cooking, cosmetics and medicine. I believe there's a magic about herbs. You can use them as teas to make someone fall in love or to ward off unwanted and worrisome energies. There are herbs to heal, herbs to bless. The combinations are limitless. I love that there are more herbs and edible flowers than I will ever know. I love how I feel when I go outside with my scissors to clip a few fresh fronds, leaves or buds, then traipse back into the kitchen and prepare the herb for its new purpose. I'm certain Mother Nature has gifted all these wonderful herbs to us. For that, I am grateful."

Gilda had walked back into the kitchen and now stood next to me in retrospective quiet making sure Rose saw how her mini lesson on herbs really made an impact on us. Finally, Gilda murmured in simple reply, "I understand."

So it was no surprise to Gilda and me when weeks later Rose sent out the email that June's supper club theme would be herbs. Responses followed with other Friends committing to a variety of herbal delights they looked forward to preparing. Gilda's email however, did not mention her contribution, instead she sent out a questionnaire.

Gilda asked us to:

1) Name the third most expensive spice. (She was certain that everyone was knowledgeable enough to know that saffron was the world's most expensive and that the vanilla bean was the second most expensive.)

2) Which herb is known as the pizza herb?

3) Describe the flavor of sorrel.

4) Which two foods are most complemented with the use of chervil?

Gilda challenged the Friends by asking them to go beyond Simon and Garfunkel's tribute to parsley, sage, rosemary and thyme by urging us to offer recipes that included the use of angelica, anise, burnet or hyssop. The gauntlet was thrown down by Gilda. Rose couldn't have been more proud.

It was one of the hottest and most humid Junes Las Vegas had ever seen. With that heat and humidity came overtaxed air conditioners that spit and sputtered, then broke down. One such air conditioner prevented two supper club members from attending since they were resigned to sitting in sweat while they waited for the repair man. There were other explanations for missing this month's supper club, such as new puppies, extended work shifts and philanthropic commitments all preventing other members from attending. Shelly was among those suffering in a house without cool air, so she was glad to get out of her "hotbox" as she referred to it. Hence, the dinner gathering based on herbs was smaller than usual, yet turned out to be a perfect offering in light fare on an unusually hot and muggy evening.

Rose decided to take advantage of this now shrinking dinner after the final of the last-minute call-offs had been received. She hurried to the garage and grabbed one of her more beautiful tapestry tablecloths. She set about spreading the tapestry in the center of her living room floor. Pausing for a moment, Rose remembered the last time she had prepared an indoor picnic for herself and one of her ex-husbands. He was Italian and to honor his heritage and the food he grew up on, Rose prepared a robust pasta Bolognese a simple salad of bitter greens and rich avocado with candied pecans. A warm baguette lavishly spread with a compound garlic butter and fresh chopped parsley. Drip candles were set on a tray and lit, allowing the colorful wax to continue decorating the old empty Chianti bottles where they were snuggly secured. All presented on this same tapestry for a romantic picnic in the middle of their living room floor. Brushing her memory aside, she placed a very large white porcelain bowl filled with greens in the center of the picnic cloth. Earlier she had prepared a compound salad which combined spring mix with a few micro-greens and chervil (one of Gilda's "challenge" herbs).

To create an even more eye-pleasing, almost watercolor effect to the contents of the bowl, Rose had picked from her garden and added edible flowers. This was a most fragrant salad that evidently called to the neighbor-hood bunnies Rose spied peering through her French doors. A light, non-acidic dressing would be prepared and sprayed onto this bountiful bouquet when it was time to serve.

Patrice, with baby Oberon in tow, Maureen and I all arrived at Rose's door at the same time and were immediately bumped behind by Gilda and Shelly. All eyes fell upon the tapestry in the middle of Rose's living room floor where juxtaposed was a large white bowl artistically overflowing with salad greens and flowers. A couple of us knew the story of Rose's last indoor picnic but said nothing. To the right of the salad were two oversized brightly glazed flower pots. Each pot stood out as if proudly displaying the large cuts of crudités jammed inside like colored straws in a malt shop glass. Crispy green spears of fresh celery and staunch sticks of carrots with rounds of whole radishes in between. Tucked into the flower pots were batik- printed napkins serving as liners, then draped over the side. A small bowl of cucumber and dill remoulade was set beside the pots ready and willing for the anticipated plunge of the crudités. I'm not sure, but as I walked over to place my bottle of wine on the dining table, I thought I saw a bunny rabbit scampering past Rose's back patio door.

"Hey! I think I just saw a bunny outside!" I burst out.

"Yes, they're all over the place around here. And they keep eating my herbs. I have half a mind to go out and catch one then cook him up. Kind of a lesson to the other bunnies."

"Rose!" scolded Gilda, "we don't eat rabbit!"

As I walked to the counter to set down my contribution and help the girls lug their dishes from cars to the house Rose filled us in on the short guest list for the evening, explaining there would only be seven of us this time.

"Can I fix anyone an herb martini? I asked. "As I recall Michael would insist we begin the evening with one, you know."

"Of course I'll have one! You used herbs in a martini?" asked Maureen.

"Indeed I did. Basil, which is related to mint, but I'm sure you already know that Maureen." I teased as I set about preparing a small pitcher of my brother's original creation, "Giardino di Vaniglia." This martini is a woodsy herbed combination of cherries, basil, vanilla-vodka and Galliano. The girls continued to busy themselves between sips and ooh's and ah's about the flavor of my cocktail.

Rose set upon the tapestry a platter of neat, square little packages, each one tied with what looked like green ribbon. I was anxious to hear about the contents wrapped inside. Maureen gave a final stir to her mixture of herbed and seasoned roasted olives, the same ones I believe I had the other night when here with Gilda and Rose. I continued to help by slicing the loaf of herbed focaccia I had purchased.

I'm here this evening once again, to record and take photos and was told to only bring bread and something to drink. The Friends were duly impressed with my martini; the bread, not so much.

Fortunately, Shelly had brought the delicate leftover hyssop flowers she had used to prepare her side dish and used them to whip up a quick compound butter she then molded the butter into individual rounds she had rolled along Rose's gnocchi board adding texture to the picture of bread and butter. Forever the artist, Shelly then went into Rose's garden and with permission, of course, picked an oversized leaf from Rose's fig tree. Placing the leaf onto a mid-sized platter, Shelly carefully placed each butter round onto the leaf. It was truly beautiful. My focaccia was pleased.

Shelly then brought out her hyssop-glazed carrots and was followed by Rose, who walked into the living room carrying a large platter upon which rested a blissfully happy whole salmon in a perfumed poaching liquid.   Patrice set her stunning dessert pies on the far side of the tapestry, as a not-so-subtle introduction to our finale.

The opened bottles of wine were set into the wine buckets as we finished off the last of our martinis.   We then comfortably seated ourselves on the picnic blanket, and Shelly poured the effervescent water infused with fresh cucumbers and lemon verbena into our water glasses.   As I sipped this much needed refreshment, I caught myself absentmindedly wiping beads of perspiration from my forehead.   I swallowed the cool jubilee of iced water and began to feel as though I was being tended to by highly-trained staff at a high-end spa.   The atmosphere of this special gathering had taken on a quality that was natural in its foundation, thanks to the herb theme, yet heady in its feel, much like The Devil Wears Prada meets Deepak Chopra and together they decided to dine in the Garden Of Eden.   There was purpose and order in Rose's kitchen and dining room, all created with what nature has gifted to us.   I realized I really did understand what Rose was expressing in her picturesque description of why she so loves using herbs.

Maureen passed around individual ramekins filled with her Lucca olives as Gilda poured the first of the white wines.   I passed out slices of the rosemary focaccia I had brought along with the platter of remedied compound butter to go with it, thanking Shelly as I did so.   The endeavor to open our taste buds with the robust flavor of the olives, bread and butter began.   A lively and informative discussion ensued regarding the symphony of herbs and spices included in the evening's menu.

"Is it coriander or cardamom that's the oldest recorded spice for culinary use?" I asked.

"It's coriander, Kevin," declared Maureen.

"Actually, I think mustard seed goes back even further.   Like about six thousand years back," countered Rose.

Of course Rose and Gilda knew it was actually oregano that's known as the pizza spice.   On the question regarding is it fish, shell fish or egg dishes that are best suited to chervil, none of the cooks in attendance that night could agree.   Needless to say, too many cooks . . .   At least all cooks present agreed that the flavor of sorrel was somewhat sour.   Well, three cooks said sour, two said bitter, another said umami.

Gilda poured more wine as Rose redirected the conversation by unwrapping the details of her bundled bites.   She told us she had prepared her herbed crepes, adhering to her theme by adding finely minced chives and fresh thyme to the batter prior to cooking.   In another pan she cooked down a mixture of butter and minced cremini, shiitake and chanterelle mushrooms.   To that she added white wine, mascarpone cheese and more fresh chives and thyme.   By now we could practically smell the aromatic blend that had gone on in Rose's sauté pan.   A pinch of fresh tarragon was added for tasteful flair and punch. Rose went on to explain she then placed a spoonful of the mushroom and herb mix in the center of each herbed crepe, then with gentle and tiny hands of a twinkling fairy she folded each filled crepe into a little square and tied the package with an edible ribbon, one strand of fresh chive. For the finish a sprinkling of her version of fairy dust, freshly grated lemon zest, over the top.

Rose didn't have much to explain regarding her garden salad. We could see for ourselves the unique combination of greens, herbs and edible flowers inviting us to inhale and taste. Gilda had prepared a very light dressing consisting of walnut oil, sunflower oil, Dijon mustard, kosher salt, a bit of freshly cracked pepper, a spoonful of raw honey and only a smidge of good French champagne vinegar. She used a spray bottle to keep the application of the dressing more like a wisp than a pour on her sister's salad.

When I asked Gilda if the dressing was her only contribution to our herb picnic was, she pointed and rebuffed, "No, my main contribution is right over there!" I turned towards the dining table to see a row of what my grandmother used to call "carnival glass" bottles. Each bottle was tall and handsome, standing erect. They looked almost like a row of polished sailors. The cuts and designs on the bottles were softened in edge by the contents they held. Gilda explained she had prepared herb-infused oils, one bottle for each of us. There was a bottle with cinnamon oil, a bottle with rosemary oil, bay leaf, basil, of course, one with garlic and lemon, caraway and for me a special blend of dill and fennel.

"I remembered how much you like fennel, Kevin," Gilda smiled. We all thanked Gilda for the stunning and useful gifts.

Maureen perked up to say the dish she brought would have benefited from one of the infused oils, if she had it to use and shared her simple preparation of her adaptation of Gilda's Mediterranean roasted olives. The featured herb? Thyme. This rich blend of Nicoise and Arbequina olives, fava

beans, fresh garlic, orange zest and thyme is not a blend of flavors to be accused of subtlety. Maureen said this mixture could just as easily be put in the food processor to make a mouth-bursting tapenade for the focaccia. We chose to keep the olives whole and as a side dish since we had the compound butter for our bread.

Somewhat comfortably sitting cross-legged on Rose's tapestry we followed our roasted olives with Rose's herbed-mushroom-filled and bundled crepes. The taste combination was complex but not the least bit overpowering. Just before plating up our individual servings Rose squeezed fresh lemon juice over the top of each crepe. This created a perfect complement to the French Sauvignon Blanc in our glasses with its naturally grassy and herbaceous flavor. We cleansed our palates with her floral and herb salad. The walnut vinaigrette with its hint of orange only worked to enhance the eye-pleasing mix of greens and color. Rose reminded us to take a moment to inhale deeply before tasting, explaining by doing so we begin the process of opening our taste buds so that we may better discern the subtle differences in taste between the edible flowers. And they did have their own individual tastes!

"Wow! You're right Rose. The nasturtiums are kind of peppery, the cornflowers have a delicate licorice flavor, the violets sweet and perfumy, and the few marigolds in here add vibrant color along with a slight citrus tone and taste," trilled Shelly.

From the salad we regressed back to the olives and bread and more wine of course. At this point we had moved on to one of my favorites, Cakebread Chardonnay, with its rich buttery foundation I decided this was the perfect complement to the olives and bread. As we received our second pour, Rose unwrapped her entrée. She had made a grand gesture in using a whole salmon. Seeing an entire fish, head and all, set the mood to one of sincere appreciation of a king's feast of natural and organic origins. Rose explained she began by rubbing the fish down so he would feel a sense of honor in giving of himself to this meal with olive oil, kosher salt, white pepper, lemon zest and fresh parsley and thyme. After this Chinook was relaxed and soothed, he was eased into the biggest casserole dish Rose could find. She then poured a bit of vegetable stock infused with culinary lavender into a large casserole dish along with a little of the Sauvignon Blanc she was drinking at the time of preparation, then into a 350-degree oven to be poached until done. The use of culinary lavender was new to me and the aromatic scent was lovely, but I couldn't help wondering if Rose's salmon would taste like perfume.

As if hearing my thoughts, Maureen stated, "I tried cooking with lavender once, and used too much I guess. My cookies tasted more like perfume than confections. Lavender is like saffron, a little goes a long way."

Shelly began serving her hyssop glazed carrots as Rose plated our portions of salmon. I first took a bite of the carrots their flavor was a strange combination of sweet from the orange marmalade she had added yet pungent from the hyssop. This created a wonderful layering of tastes when eaten immediately after a bite of the fish. I could detect the hyssop leaves have a character that is rather strong and sharp but combined with the natural sweetness of carrots, marmalade and the honey, chicken broth and butter Shelly used, the combination became nectarean. But Rose's salmon was the biggest surprise of the meal for me. How in the world she came up with a such an interesting blending of ingredients in which to poach fish, I'll never know. But true to form, Rose's uncanny ability to mix and match ingredients resulting in delectable dishes remains unsurpassed.

Before dessert the foodie Friends and I took a few minutes to venture out into Rose's garden as all were interested in seeing what new plantings she had begun. Rose is as meticulous in her gardening as she is in her cooking, and her efforts always pay off. Gilda, on the other hand, is a rather nonchalant gardener, preferring instead to simply broadcast seed. Her garden is as full and robust with edibles and tropical flowers as her sister's. I take a few more pictures outside then make use of myself by clearing the tapestry in preparation of dessert. The girls filed back in refreshed and excited to hear about Patrice's pies. She prepared two pies, actually one was a galette the other a more traditional tart.

"So what's the difference between a pie and a tart?" I inquired as I admired her efforts.

"A tart is very simply, a pastry crust prepared in a shallow "tart" pan of any size or shape. These pans usually have a removable bottom, for easy serving. Like pies, tarts can also be topped with a sweet or savory filling. Pies are prepared in dishes without removable bottoms," explained Patrice smiling as I drooled.

"So then, what's a galette?"

"Really it's a tart, it just isn't prepared in a pan with a removable bottom. It's prepared with a crust that is folded over the filling in a very relaxed and rustic manner," Patrice went on. "Can be confusing right?" chimed in Rose from the kitchen. "Do you know the difference between a galette and a crostada?" she asked as she made her back to the tapestry.

"They're the same thing. Galettes are French, crostadas are Italian," pronounced Gilda.

Patrice had prepared her adaptation of a strawberry galette with basil cream. This galette was a buttery crust loosely formed into that rustic round encasing an abundant filling of freshly sliced, vibrant, juicy strawberries. The basil cream was a mixture of fresh basil chopped then combined with heavy cream, sugar and mascarpone cheese. For the tart, Patrice again referred to her guru of desserts by preparing her adaptation of a Blackberry and Basil tart. Patrice's personal touch on the tart was her use of fried basil for garnish. A most difficult task she explained. The blackberries were bathed in a thin layer of crème fraiche, lemon zest, vanilla bean, bakers sugar and sour cream. It was amazing.

"I'm not sure you girls will like this tart. I think I should just eat the whole myself," I crowed. The sweet cornmeal crust Patrice made then topped with my favorite of berries, was sublime. I ended up sharing after all, but both desserts offered a balance of fresh fruit, herbs, and creams and were redolent in flavor. Silky rich and freshly sweet were the adjectives that came to mind as I enjoyed these herbal delights.

We finished our garden party with sips of hot carminative tea Rose said would aide in digestion. She explained she had prepared a basic green tea, then sweetened the tea with a fennel infused simple syrup. Perfection.

I took the last of my photos and packed my equipment to leave, thinking how easy it was for me to now adopt Rose's appreciation of what Mother Nature has to offer us in the simplicity and abundance of her herbs.

The following morning as I sat reviewing my pictures from this meal, it appeared as though there was too much food for a spring picnic. In actuality, the excess came in the variation of flavors that were both out of place and completely at home in their pots and casserole dishes. Somehow it all came together in harmony, as we consumed each dish in slow and savored movements, as though our meal was orchestrated by a most talented and sensitive conductor. The food was light and lively,

and of course, the portions small, only four ounces each, yet satisfying. At meal's end I felt happy, not fat and happy, just happy.

Microgreens Salad with Edible Flowers and Walnut Vinaigrette

Ingredients for Salad:

1 cup delicate or tender salad greens, such as frisée, lamb's lettuce (or mâche), butter or Boston lettuce

1/2 cup microgreens - any combination you can find or enjoy

1/2 cup edible flowers - any combination you can find

Note: These must edible flowers cultivated for culinary use only.

Ingredients for Walnut Vinaigrette:

1 tablespoon Dijon mustard

1/2 cup champagne vinegar

1/2 cup walnut oil

Salt and pepper to taste

1 tablespoon minced shallot

1/4 cup extra virgin olive oil

1/2 cup walnut bits - lightly toasted

Preparation for Salad:

Gently wash tender greens by placing them in a bowl of clean water and using your hands to move greens around in the water. To dry them, place on a clean kitchen towel, fold towel over the top and gently press down to absorb water from greens. Place in serving bowl.

Using your hands, gently mix in microgreens and flowers.

Preparation for Vinaigrette:

In a small mixing bowl whisk together mustard, shallot and vinegar.

Continue whisking as you slowly drizzle in olive oil and walnut oil, creating a smooth emulsion.

Season to taste with salt and pepper.

To Serve the Salad: Arrange mixed greens on individual plates, drizzle each with a small amount of vinaigrette and top with toasted walnut bits.

Makes four 4-ounce servings

Hyssop-Glazed Carrots

Hyssop, a relative to the mint family, has been utilized for culinary purposes for a very long time. There are at least two references for use of hyssop in the Bible. Native Americans have been recorded to using hyssop for medicinal purposes as an ingredient in mixtures used to heal cuts and scars. Hyssop has a slightly bitter kind of licorice/minty taste. The plant itself grows relatively tall attracting bees and butterflies with its pretty bluish-purple flowers. This herb is quite aromatic so a little goes a long way. You may have to search for it, or better yet, grow your own.

Ingredients:

2 tablespoons unsalted butter

¼ cup orange marmalade

Salt and pepper to taste

1/4 cup vegetable broth

2 tablespoons light brown sugar

1/2 teaspoon culinary hyssop*

1 pound carrots - cleaned, trimmed and sliced in rounds (you may use uncut baby carrots)

> **Note:* It's best to use the leaves minced then add the flowers just prior to serving.

Preparation:

1) Melt butter in saucepot. Add carrots, marmalade, brown sugar and broth.

2) Bring to a gentle boil, then immediately reduce heat.

3) Stir in hyssop leaves, salt and pepper. Continue cooking over low simmer until water is reduced and carrots are slightly tender.

4) Pour into serving bowl/dish and gently fold in hyssop flowers.

Makes four 4-ounce servings

Herb and Mushroom Filled Crepes

Ingredients for Crepes:

1 cup half and half

3 large eggs

1 cup all-purpose flour

2 teaspoons fine sugar

1/8 cup chopped tarragon

Strands of chives for wrapping bundles

1/2 cup vegetable broth

1/4 teaspoon kosher salt

2 teaspoons unsalted butter - melted

1/8 cup chopped chives

1/4 cup chopped flat parsley

Butter or grapeseed oil for crepe pan

Ingredients for Filling:

1/2 cup each: minced shiitake, portobello, oyster mushrooms

2 shallots - minced

1teaspoon olive oil

2 tablespoons mascarpone cheese

1 teaspoon minced fresh flat parsley

salt and pepper to taste

2 teaspoons unsalted butter

1/2 cup dry white wine

1 teaspoon minced fresh chives

1 teaspoon minced fresh tarragon

zest and juice from 1 fresh lemon

Preparation for Crepes:

1) In large mixing bowl whisk together half and half, broth, eggs and salt.

2) Vigorously whisk in the flour, melted butter and herbs and mix until batter is thin and smooth. Absolutely no lumps. Cover batter and refrigerate at least 1 hour.

3) When ready to use the batter should be similar in consistency to a light cream, just thick enough to coat the back of your spoon. Cook your crepes first, setting them on parchment or silpat lined baking sheet with an additional sheet of parchment paper between them. Don't stack crepes on top of one another.

4) To cook your crepes, heat an 8-inch non-stick skillet lightly rubbed with unsalted butter or grape-seed oil. Heat skillet over medium heat then using a 4-ounce ice cream scoop or ladle 4 ounces of batter into heated skillet.

5) Lift and tilt skillet in a circular motion coating pan with a thin film. Cook crepe about 1 minute on first side. Center should be set and other side lightly browned. Then flip using a soft silicone spatula. Cook about 15 seconds on second side and place on lined baking sheet. Repeat process for each crepe. Allow crepes to sit covered while you prepare filling.

Preparation for Filling

1) Clean mushrooms by gently brushing with paper towels (no water as that adds unwanted moisture). If your mushrooms are particularly dirty, you may clean under running water just be sure to dry them well.

2) Melt butter with olive oil in large skillet over medium heat. Add shallots and mushrooms, cooking until mushrooms release their natural moisture, about 7 minutes.

3) Add white wine and continue cooking until liquid has reduced by half.

4) Remove skillet from heat and stir cheese, herbs and seasonings.

5) Spoon 2 ounces of mushroom/herb mixture into the center of crepe. Fold edges of crepe over creating a closed square package. Turn folded side under as the bottom and tie bundle closed with one strand of fresh chive.

6) Repeat procedure for remaining crepes.

Makes twelve 4-ounce servings

Lavender Poached Salmon

Ingredients:

1/4 cup unsalted butter

4 salmon steaks - 4 ounces each

1 cup fish or vegetable broth

1 cup water

1 tablespoon culinary lavender

1 red onion - sliced

1 tablespoon each, olive oil/butter

1 fresh lemon - sliced

1/4 teaspoon each, kosher salt and black pepper

Sprigs of fresh dill for garnish

Preparation: Preheat oven to 350 degrees

1) Generously grease the bottom of a 9 x 13 oven-proof dish with unsalted butter.

2) Season the salmon steaks with salt and pepper and place in prepared pan.

3) Pour broth and water into pan - add lavender.

4) Poach salmon in liquid in preheated oven for 12 - 15 minutes or until internal temperature of fish is 145 degrees.

5) While fish is poaching - heat olive oil and butter in medium skillet. When oil is hot add sliced onions and sauté until caramelized, about 15 minutes.

6) Remove poached salmon with a large slotted spatula from pan and place on serving platter. Top with fresh lemon slices, caramelized onions and dill sprigs.

Makes four 4-ounce servings

All American Barbeque - July

"Does Maureen have any bacon fat?" Rose asked Jimmy as she stepped out of her car and lightly brushed a kiss against his cheek.

"Only you would offer that as a greeting, Rose," teased Jimmy.

Together, Rose and Jim carried the heavy coolers and grocery bags from her car to Maureen's delightfully air-conditioned home. Summer in Las Vegas that July was extremely hot, even by the local's standard. As Gilda pulled her car up alongside her sister's, she couldn't help squinting from the glare, even behind her dark sunglasses. Looking out over the hood of her car, the gray, white and pale pink concrete and stucco of Maureen's neighborhood was sparkling, but was uncomfortably blinding as it reflected the shimmering sun above.

"Oh good, you're here. Help Jimmy and me with these bags, would you Gilda?" directed Rose.

Gilda helped carry one of the four grocery bags, then with Rose and Jim found an as yet unoccupied spot on the kitchen counter to set it down. She immediately plopped herself down next to Nina, Jim's wife.

"You look hot, Gilda, observed Nina. "Can I get you a glass of water?"

"She is hot," announced Jim as planted a kiss on Gilda's cheek.

"Yes! Please," replied Gilda. "And thank you Jimmy. You're looking pretty good these days yourself."

Nina returned to the sofa with a refreshing glass of raspberry and mint infused iced water. Gilda immediately drank it down as Nina sat down next to her. The two longtime friends began a conversation about Nina and Jim's recent trip to North Carolina leaving Jim and Rose to rummage through the back of Maureen's refrigerator in search of the much-coveted bacon fat.

"Oh, there it is!" cried Rose.

"How did you know that was the bacon fat?" asked Jim. "This is your first visit to Maureen's new house. And you've never been in her refrigerator before."

"Every good cook has a small bowl or juice can of bacon fat waaay in the back of the fridge. Maureen is no exception!" exclaimed Rose as she smiled over her shoulder at Maureen, who was busy directing me on which shots to take with my camera.

Rose began excitedly unwrapping and setting up the many ingredients of her supper club contribution, paella. Jim stood close by following Rose's instructions on setting up mise en place, finding bowls and making room on what little space was left on the counter. The doorbell rang and within minutes Maureen's house was copiously filled with Friends and food. There was much to do and all were keen to get to their respective last minute preparations.

Following Colin and Jonah's arrival, Rose and Diana prepared themselves for the All American Barbeque supper club theme. They were armed and dangerous with hats, sunglasses and sunscreen as they made their way towards the back patio. Gilda, forever the supporting sister, slowly slid the glass patio door open as Rose carried her weighted paella pan, stacked with the required supplies, as though it were a gladiator's shield. Rose's weapons of choice: shellfish, chicken, Italian sausage, peppers, a short grain rice she had said was best for paella, Bomba, vegetable broth and saffron.

Gilda continued to hold the patio door open just slightly as Diana squeezed through carrying a battalion of long-handled barbeque tools and an assault tray of herb-spiked polenta squares. Backup was provided by her husband Stanley, Sophie and Kyle. All bore arms in the form of oversized outdoor tumblers filled to the brim with cool home-brewed beer, Jim's latest batch prepared just for this occasion. As they stepped outside, Rose and Diana were immediately hit by a wave of heat so intense it was nearly unbearable were it not for the quick thinking maneuvers of their backup team pouring gulps of beer down their throats.

Gilda and Nina watched this unrehearsed exercise, as they had moved outside and were now calmly sitting in the shade provided by the eaves of the roof and the two patio umbrellas Maureen had set out. Sophie and Kyle were sipping the white sangria Nina had prepared while inhaling the intoxicating aroma of Jim's chickens. There were three.

"Kevin, you gotta get pictures of these chickens," coaxed Jim.

One bird sat in the smoker soaking up the essence of the wood chips Jim had carefully and deliberately blended and soaked. The other bird showed off her glistening butter-and herb-rubbed skin with pride as she turned ever-so-slowly on a spit that sat on the far side of the pool. The last bird waited beneath the hood of a small Weber, quietly and shyly roasting herself over indirect coals. This fanciful fowl was allowing the spicy Cajun rub to seep into her soon-to-be crisp skin. It seemed as though, in no uncertain terms, each bird believed she would be the one to claim the title as "superlicious" at our dining table. The calming effects of the cooking birds along with the sangria and the fact that it was just too damn hot to stand, caused the backup team to retreat to chairs under the umbrellas and congregate together in relaxed merriment. Rose and Diana remained upright on two legs, now able to hold their own drinks. They stood, almost propping each other up by the large gas grill, adding the goods one by one to Rose's paella.

"My polenta will grill up quickly, so that can go on later," called out Diana. Meanwhile, Jim had set a plate next to the grill with a small amount of olive oil and half of a large red onion with which to prepare the grate so Diana wouldn't have to worry about any of her precious ingredients sticking.

"So let's see that ring," commanded Diana to Sophie.

The conversation picked up regarding the upcoming nuptials of Sophie and Kyle as Sophie showed off her stunning and uniquely-designed engagement ring.

"Kyle told me he came up with the design of that ring himself," Gilda told Nina.

"Wow, it's beautiful. Vintage, Sophie's preferred style," replied Nina.

The Friends agreed among themselves, they were an exceptional group of talented and creative people. Sophie and Kyle stated they were trying to decide on whether or not having a ceremony in Napa California was suiting since neither of them had any family living there.

"It's just so beautiful there. The ocean, the vineyards and there are several quaint and romantic bed and breakfasts to stay," reasoned Sophie.

"Makes it a travel wedding, but you guys are worth traveling for," remarked Jonah.

"What about the food? Have you given any thought caterers out there?" asked Rose.

"We're looking into that right now," answered Kyle. "Do any of you know caterers up there?"

In the brief moment of silence that followed that question (and the intense heat caused the conversations to slow), Colin, sitting poolside next to Jonah, both with feet dangling in the pool, asked the obvious. "Who needs a caterer when you have us? We'll do a supper club for the wedding."

"We can prepare the food it'll be a wedding theme!" Jonah shouted.

"We'll definitely know the food will be good. And think about how much money you'll save!"

chimed in Colin. "What do you guys think?"

It was settled: a Napa wedding with all the Friends Amid Food preparing food made perfect sense. In the next minute Patrice and Bryant with their now one-year-old son, Oberon, walked outside to join the group.

"Oberon? Isn't that a character from another Shakespearian play?" Gilda inquired.

"Yes, A Midsummer Night's Dream, answered Bryant.

"You're just now asking that question? teased Rose. "Of all people you should know Shakespeare's works. You better not let our mother know you had to ask that."

"I guess Shakespearian types like to hang out and cook together," added Jim.

"Gilda, your glass is empty. Would you like more sangria?" asked Nina.

"No thank you. My mind will wander even further if I drink too much in this heat," Gilda replied.

Chef Bryant noticed the effect the heat was having on those who were drinking and not yet eating. "I think some of us need to add some food to our drink!" he announced. "Rose has decided to let me share the grill with her, so I'll have our appetizers of grilled Portobello mushroom sliders ready in a jiff!"

And with that, each Friend was presented with two meaty Portobello mushroom, melted Gruyere cheese, fresh arugula and garlic aioli sliders served up on small red, white and blue paper plates. With my camera in hand, I was up in two seconds doing what I do best - recording the supper club events.

"Kevin, do you want one of these?" Bryant asked me.

"I want more than one," I replied.

It wasn't long before all the grilling, smoking and spit-turning was done and we were gathered back into the cool relief of Maureen's dining room. Set upon her small table was yet more dishes representing a feast fit for kings. In my opinion, it's likely Macbeth, Hamlet and King Lear would have approved and delighted in these offerings. With the spread set before us, my Friends were ever ready to indulge, but not until the traditional amount of time was taken to introduce and acknowledge the efforts and talents of those in attendance.

Five of us dove into the paella first. And it was sumptuous, with fresh squeezed lime and freshly chopped parsley adding a bright finish to a dish laden with chicken, sausage, shellfish and seafood. Rose prepared this Spanish dish in the traditional manner, using a wide, shallow round pan over an open fire.

Diana's Italian grilled polenta was prepared as tasty squares of firm cornmeal, Asiago cheese, cream and fresh herbs lightly grilled. The calm of Diana's polenta was offset by the impetuous flavor of Chef's fiery Mexican potato salad, a combination of Red Bliss potatoes, celery, white onion, mayonnaise, garlic and mustard.   The ethnicity of this American side dish came from his addition of cayenne pepper and fresh chopped jalapeno.

Colin and Jonah somehow found a spot on the gas grill to cook up the freshly caught halibut and trout given to them by one of their employees at the store. "Keeping fresh food simple in

preparation is key," Jonah declared between bites of fish and fowl. He had chosen to season his fish with only kosher salt, pepper, butter and lemon thus maintaining the integrity of the fresh halibut. Color and flair for his dish came from two choices of relish toppings, one a sweet-spicy Caribbean fruit relish for the halibut, the other a garlicky roasted red pepper relish for the trout.

Meanwhile, someone had brought a loaf of San Francisco sourdough which provided a perfect way for us to soak up the delectable juices of the three bathing beauties of fowl. One type of bird prepared in the out-of-doors in three very different ways. Once again, Jim had outdone himself: French-Cajun, Texas-smoked and herb-butter.

The yums, ums and lip smacking were only drowned out by the mouthfuls of questions about recipes and how-to's. Some had moved on from alcohol to Maureen's selection of herb-infused waters and continued to enjoy one another's company, allowing time to digest our supper.

It wasn't much later when Sophie and Maureen stood up to bear the even hotter weather to grill the sweet, fresh peaches Sophie had purchased at the farmer's market earlier that morning. Lightly brushed with a butter and brown sugar glaze while on the grill readied these Persian apples as they waited for their dessert companion, freshly churned crème fraiche ice cream. This was a wonderful marriage of smoky-sweet and rich creaminess.

Every bite of this dish gave the tongue a Mona Lisa kind of twist as did our entire meal. We enjoyed serene sweetness mixed with sly spice, rich flavors chased by bright finishes, extra crispy danced smooth and crunchy frolicked with tender. It was all there.

Gilda sat holding her sturdy paper plate, with what little remained of uneaten barbeque, her eyes scanning the broad selection of ethnic foods the Friends had included in this all American barbeque. She mused to herself, as she had been doing all afternoon, that this meal really was all American. This supper club had offered up the very best of American cuisine, a melting pot of flavors derived from the melting pot of nationalities that comprise America. How very clever of her Friends she thought, smiling. They blended the subtleties and nuances of what makes America great, the amalgamation of different countries and regions, the honoring of culinary traditions and the freedom to share all of it with one another. This was an extraordinary meal prepared by extraordinary people

What the Friends didn't know, as they finished the cleanup together and said their goodbyes, was that this was to be their final supper club gathering. No one knew then, as we munched our way through charred and smoked delicacies that in a few short months, Colin and Jonah would receive an offer to open a second kitchen shop with a demonstration kitchen back East.

Or that the very next month Maureen would accept an even better job in Southern California. How could they not be happy for her as she gushed on about the beaches and plethora of prime produce available at the local farmer's markets? No one knew that by sheer chance during a vacation/scouting expedition Shelly would finally fulfill her long-time dream of opening her own second-hand clothing business in Costa Rica. Certainly no one ever thought their very talented Chef Bryant, Patrice and Oberon would ever leave Las Vegas and move to Rose and Gilda's old stomping grounds, the San Francisco Bay Area. Bryant would be taking his special gift of food preparation and the calmest of professional kitchen demeanors any of us had ever known with him. No one ever considered until the actual time came, that Sophie and Kyle would follow through on their secret promise to each other and move to Germany, before getting married.

Grilled Polenta

Ingredients:

1 cup water	1 cup vegetable broth
2 cups yellow cornmeal	2 teaspoons kosher salt
½ cup half and half	3/4 cup grated parmesan cheese
2 tablespoons unsalted butter	1 teaspoon ground pepper
1/4 cup good balsamic vinegar	additional parmesan cheese - grated

additional rosemary and parsley for garnish

1 teaspoon each, fresh rosemary and parsley - stems removed, chopped

Preparation:

1) In a small bowl whisk together the water and 1 cup of the cornmeal, making a thick paste.

2) In a large saucepot, bring vegetable broth and salt to a gentle boil over medium heat.

3) Stir in cornmeal-water mixture and whisk just until mixture begins to boil again.

4) Reduce heat to simmer whisking in remaining cup of cornmeal, half and half, parmesan cheese, pepper and 1 tablespoon of the butter. Continue cooking until mixture becomes, thick and creamy, about 10 minutes.

5) Stir in the measured rosemary and parsley. Add remaining tablespoon of butter.

6) Grease well, an 8" x 8" square pan.

7) Pour prepared polenta into pan and allow to cool to room temperature.

8) Cover with plastic wrap and chill in refrigerator for at least 2 hours.

9) When polenta has become firm, cut into equal segments using a square or round cookie cutter. Place cut out servings on a parchment lined cookie sheet.

10) To grill, simply grill individual polenta servings on heated grill over non-direct heat until edges are crisp and polenta is wearing grill marks, about 3 minutes on each side. Meanwhile, pour balsamic vinegar into a small saucepot and cook over medium heat until reduced by half. When ready to serve, drizzle a small amount of balsamic over each polenta serving and top with reserved herbs and parmesan for garnish.

Makes eight 4-ounce servings

Portobello Mushroom Sliders

Ingredients:

1/2 cup good mayonnaise

1/4 cup good catsup

3-4 cloves fresh garlic - minced

3 tablespoons olive oil

3 tablespoons balsamic vinegar

1 cup fresh arugula

4 slices provolone cheese

1/8 teaspoon ground pepper

1/4 teaspoon kosher salt

3 tablespoons Worcestershire sauce

8 baby Portobello mushrooms - brushed clean and stems removed

8 small dinner rolls (I prefer the Hawaiian rolls for this recipe since they are so tasty and already cut in half)

Preparation:

1) In small mixing bowl, combine mayonnaise, catsup and garlic - taste to ensure flavor is to your liking. Set aside until ready to use

2) In large mixing bowl whisk together, olive oil, balsamic vinegar, Worcestershire sauce, salt and pepper.

3) Add Portobello mushrooms to mixture and allow to marinate for 1-3 minutes.

4) Meanwhile heat outdoor grill or indoor grill pan - lightly greased with olive oil.

5) Using a slotted spoon remove mushrooms from marinade and place on grill for about 3-5 minutes on each side.

6) Add one slice of provolone cheese to second side of each mushroom.

7) Prepare bread rolls by lightly coating each side of roll with the garlic-mayonnaise aioli.

8) Place one mushroom with melted cheese on bottom half of each roll, top with a handful of arugula and the top half other half of roll.

Makes eight 4-ounce servings

Spicy Potato Salad

Ingredients:

2 pounds Red Bliss potatoes - roasted

3-4 tablespoons olive oil

Salt and pepper to taste

3 stalks celery - diced

1 large white onion - diced

1-2 cups good mayonnaise

1 teaspoon dried thyme

1 teaspoon garlic powder

1 large jalapeno pepper - seeds and stems removed - minced

Zest of one lime

1/2 bunch flat parsley - chopped

1/3 cup chopped cilantro

1-2 tablespoons capers

1/8 teaspoon cayenne pepper

1/2 teaspoon mustard powder

1 teaspoon onion powder

Preparation: Preheat oven to 375 degrees

1) Cut clean, dried potatoes into bite-sized pieces and spread in a single layer on 1 or 2 cookie sheets. Drizzle lightly with the olive oil then sprinkle generously with salt and pepper.

2) Place potatoes in pre-heated oven and roast until edges are browned and potatoes are crispy, about 30-45 minutes.

3) While potatoes are roasting combine celery, onion, mayonnaise, garlic powder, onion powder, mustard powder, dried thyme and cayenne pepper in a large mixing bowl.

4) When potatoes are done roasting, allow them to cool then gently fold into large bowl with other ingredients.

5) Gently fold in minced jalapeno, capers and cilantro

6) Season to taste with salt and pepper - top with lime zest and chopped parsley.

Makes twelve 4-ounce servings

Grilled Trout with Roasted Garlic and Red Pepper Relish

Ingredients for Fish:

2 whole fresh trout - cleaned and de-scaled

1 teaspoon each - kosher salt and ground pepper

2 cloves fresh garlic - minced

2-4 sprigs each - rosemary and thyme

2 tablespoons olive oil - divided

1 lemon - sliced

1/2 red onion - thinly sliced

Ingredients for Relish:

1-2 tablespoons olive oil

4 cloves fresh garlic

1 large red bell pepper - seed and ribs removed, then roughly chopped

1/4 cup chicken broth

Salt and pepper to taste

Preparation for Fish: For oven roasting- preheat to 375 degrees

1) In a small mixing bowl combine 1 tablespoon of the oil, salt, pepper and minced garlic.

2) Generously massage this mixture on both sides of fish, including the inside.

3) Gently place 2 lemon slices, onion slices and half the herbs in cavity of both fish.

4) Grill on prepared grill until skins are brown and meat of fish flakes easily - about 5-7 minutes per side.

5) Garnish with fresh lemon slices and remaining herb sprigs on the side.

Preparation for Relish:

1) For oven roasting, on a foil or parchment lined cookie sheet spread chunks of bell pepper and drizzle garlic cloves with foil then wrap garlic only in foil and place on same baking sheet. Drizzle peppers with olive oil and season with salt and pepper. Roast in oven until pepper pieces and garlic cloves have softened and caramelized - about 20-30 minutes. For roasting on the grill, cut pepper in half after removing the seeds and ribs rub with olive oil and place directly on grill grate. Using your tongs to turn pepper as it chars. To roast the garlic, follow the same process above by drizzling with olive oil, season with salt and pepper, then wrap loosely in foil and place on grill for about 15-20 minutes until soft and fragrant.

2) Using a food processor or blender combine roasted bell pepper, roasted garlic, and broth and process until you have a smooth paste.

3) Taste for additional salt and pepper if needed.

4) Place a dollop of relish on each serving of fish.

Grilled Peaches and Mascarpone Ice Cream

Ingredients for Ice Cream:

4 egg yolks

2 cup half and half

3/4 cup + 2 tablespoons fine grain sugar - Baker's sugar

1/2 teaspoon fresh lemon zest

7 ounces mascarpone cheese

Pinch of salt

Ingredients for Grilled Peaches:

2 cups brandy

1 cup water

4 large, ripe peaches - pitted and halved

2 tablespoons honey

1/4 cup Baker's sugar

1 bunch fresh rosemary

Preparation:

1) In large mixing bowl whisk together egg yolk and 3/4 cup of the Baker's sugar until pale yellow in color and fluffy - about 5-7 minutes.

2) In large saucepot over low heat, combine half and half with remaining 2 tablespoons sugar and bring to a gentle simmer.

3) Temper the egg mixture by ladling 2-4 tablespoons of the warm milk mixture into the egg mixture.

4) Slowly whisk all egg mixture into the milk, stirring constantly to avoid cooking the egg - cook until mixture has thickened and coats the back of a wooden spoon. Do not allow custard to boil.

5) When custard has thickened pour into a clean bowl and whisk in mascarpone, lemon zest and salt. Place in refrigerator for at least 30-45 minutes.

6) Pour custard into ice cream machine and follow manufacturers' directions for making ice cream.

7) About 1-2 hours prior to serving, while ice cream freezes, combine brandy, honey water and sugar in a large saucepot and bring to a gentle boil. Reduce heat, drop in 1 or 2 sprigs of the rosemary to infuse flavor and allow liquid to reduce by half - about 30 minutes.

8) When you are ready to grill the fruit, first allow brandy mixture to cool and remove rosemary sprigs - brush both sides of peach halves with brandy mixture.

9) Heat grill and generously prepare grate with oil to prevent fruit from sticking.

10) Place peach halves on grill, basting with brandy mixture and turning occasionally until peaches are lightly browned and grill marks show.

11) Scoop prepared ice cream into 4 individual bowls and top each serving with grilled peaches.

Makes four 4-ounce servings

The Great American Barbeque would be the last of the supper club meetings for the Friends Amid Food. I arrived at Rose's door in late October of that year with the assembled collection of supper club photographs I had taken. The evening was crisp and the scent of peppered steaks and buttery Potatoes Anna filled the air. Rose and Gilda sat huddled under blankets, sipping Rose's Shaker herb soup from heavy mugs and immediately nodded to indicate where my mug of soup and glass of wine waited for me. We reminisced about their Friends, the recipes, the flavors and unique food themes. How their monthly supper clubs provided robust opportunities for a set of twin sisters with very different approaches to food, with experiences they would never had considered had it not been for the creativity and risk taking of those Friends. I said I was honored to be invited to the few I attended.

But the best part of all, Gilda explained to us, was learning she did not have to give up her love of food; regional, ethnic, gourmet or simple. Even after weight loss surgery, through supper club she inadvertently discovered the tremendous importance of making sure her four-ounce servings consistently offer her satisfying taste and pleasing esthetic presentation. It has always been her sister's philosophy to engineer the finest meals by using the very best ingredients then blend them together with genuine care and respect. Now both Gilda and I understand cooking as the art it truly is. No longer is Gilda relegated to eating low-fat, low-calorie foods with zero taste and texture like cardboard. She now knows and I've seen for myself that a One 4-Ounce Serving can be an utterly delightful thing.